POLENTA

Polenta

Over 40 Recipes for All Occasions

by Brigit Légère Binns

Photography by Deborah Denker

CHRONICLE BOOKS

SAN FRANCISCO

FOR GREG, WIGGY, AND HILDA
....

Library of Congress Cataloging-in-Publication Data:

Binns, Brigit Légère.

    Polenta: over 40 recipes for all occasions/Brigit Légère Binns; photographs by Deborah Denker.

      p. cm.

    Includes index.

    ISBN 0-8118-1185-9 (pbk.)

    1. Polenta. I. Title.

TX809.M2B56 1996

641.6'315–dc20   95-49897

                                     CIP

Book and cover design by Pamela Geismar
Food styling by Claire Stancer
Printed in Hong Kong

Distributed in Canada by Raincoast Books
9050 Shaughnessy Street
Vancouver, B.C. V6P 6E5

10 9 8 7 6 5

Chronicle Books LLC
85 Second Street
San Francisco, CA 94105

www.chroniclebooks.com

The photographer wishes to thank: Aletha Soule-Loom Company, New York; Cottura, Los Angeles; Hands Gallery, San Luis Obispo; Meridian, San Luis Obispo; Morro Bay Antiques; Paradeisos, San Luis Obispo; Room with the View, Santa Monica; Ralph Seal & Associates, Los Angeles; San Luis Obispo Marble and Granite; Traditions, San Luis Obispo.

Acknowledgments

My biggest thanks go to two people without whom there would have been no book:
    Ellen Rose, whose suggestion put the whole thing in motion,
    and Ronda Kamihira, whose gifted assistance at the midpoint provided inspiration and direction

      And also thanks:
        to Frank Ternay, for convincing me that I really could
        to Laurie Burrows Grad, for giving me the first big break
        to Joachim and Christine, for their confidence in me
        to Diane Worthington, for teaching me to be a stickler for accuracy
        and to Evan Kleiman, for keeping me under her wing until I was ready to fly

        And to some of the most important people in my life
        and the unforgettable food memories that go with them:
          to Mom, for cheese soufflé in Brentwood
          to Laird, for peaches on Skyros
          to Jean Richardson, for homemade ravioli in Oklahoma City
          to Geoffrey, for perfect roast beef in Hampstead and all those dinners in France
          to Michael and Jane for Maine lobsters in Marbella
          and to Dad and Liz, for the geese (sorry about the ovens)

And last, but not least, to my agent, Maureen Lasher, for pep talks, tea, and sympathy;
    and to Leslie Jonath, my first but undoubtedly best always editor.

      To the talented testers and all the tasters—your input was invaluable:
      Testers: Mary Enright, Marcia Legere, Joan Nielsen, Christopher Pelham
      Tasters: Darla Bonnaire, Jacqueline Callendar, Sheila Davis, Elizabeth Franz, Paul Hargrave, Richard
      Hatem, Suzanne Huffaker, Christina Lazzaro, Sandy Sherman, Caren, Alan, and Dereck Smith

Contents

Introduction   8
A Polenta Primer   12
Secrets for Success   15

Breakfast and Brunch   22

Polenta with Poached Eggs, Smoked Salmon, and Chives
Fried Polenta Squares with Golden Raisins and Maple Syrup
Skillet Cornbread with Corn, Bacon, and Jack Cheese
Apple and Dried Cherry Fritters
Polentina with Bananas and Clover Honey
Pancakes with Blueberries and Crème Fraîche
Cinnamon Popovers (Apple Compote)
Sautéed Polenta Rounds with Prune-Kumquat Compote

First Courses and
Hors d'Oeuvres   36

Rosemary-Olive Pizzettas with Prosciutto
Crabmeat Polenta with Lemon and Chive Sauce
Baked Polenta with Eggplant, Sun-dried Tomatoes, and Basil Sauce
Baby Greens with Blood Oranges and Sage-Prosciutto Polenta Croutons
Soft Polenta with White Truffles and Crème Fraîche
Grilled Polenta Crostini with Smoked Trout and Mascarpone
Wild Mushroom Ragout
Deep-fried Polenta Sandwiches with Spinach and Gorgonzola
Polenta with Shiitake Mushrooms, Mascarpone, and Salmon Roe
Lentils and Greens in Broth with Polenta Croutons
Cabbage-wrapped Torta with Leeks and Pancetta
Gorgonzola Puffs

Duck Breasts with Port Sauce and Wild Mushroom Polenta
Soft Polenta with Braised Italian Sausage, Oven-roasted Tomatoes,
and Swiss Chard
Lamb and Artichoke Stew with Oregano Polenta Dumplings
Braised Beef Short Ribs over Soft Polenta with Thyme
Bricked Game Hens with Savoy Cabbage on Polenta Croûtes   Main Attractions   62
Skewered Chicken Livers, Bacon, and Mushrooms over Polenta Squares
Polenta Lasagne with Spinach, Zucchini, Herbs, and Fontina
Pan-fried Trout with Crunchy Polenta Crust
Chicken Pot Pie with Cornmeal Crust
Venison Medallions on Cranberry-Orange Polenta Diamonds

Sage Polenta Gnocchi
Fennel-Chèvre Polenta Wedges
Herbed Polenta Cornsticks
Lemon and Oregano Polenta Muffins   Asides   89
Pan-fried Tomatoes with a Cornmeal Crust
Garlic-Onion Grilled Polenta Squares
Three-Cheese Soft Polenta
White Corn and Arugula Timbales
Röckenwagner's Polenta Fries
Fennel Seed and Rosemary Breadsticks

Wine-poached Pears on Spicy Polenta Croûtes
Polenta Pound Cake with Warm Summer Fruits   Desserts   106
Polenta Dolce with Dried Dates and Ricotta
Cornmeal Tart with Plums and Currants

Bibliography   116
Mail-Order Sources   117
Index   118
Table of Equivalents   120

Introduction

More than thirty thrushes were seated
in superb majesty on the polenta,
like Turks on a divan   *Lorenzo Stecchetti*

POLENTA HAS NOT ALWAYS BEEN A MAJESTIC FOOD. IN FACT, FOR GENERA-tions of Italians it was known as the "meat of the poor." Without this simple staple, many northern Italian peasants and soldiers might have starved. Because of its history as a life-saving staple, polenta occupies a special place in the hearts of Italians, and although it is now often treated as a delicacy, its humble past will never be forgotten.

Every year on the last Tuesday of Carnevale in Tossignano, Emilia-Romagna, the village cooks boil up huge cauldrons of water, to which they add some 440 pounds of polenta and, later, vast quantities of sausages and tomatoes. Villagers and visitors feast on the results to commemorate the day in 1622 when a local duke gave free polenta to famine-stricken peasants of the region. In Lombardy, in the far north of Italy, during the second week of February polenta is distributed along with salami and wine in another festival of thanksgiving. All over Italy, similar festivals cherish and celebrate this staple food of the poor.

Polenta in History

THE ROMANS' MAIN SOURCE OF NOURISHMENT WAS A MUSHY PORRIDGE called *pulmentum*, which was made from ground wheat or millet and garnished with whatever meat or vegetable could be found. When Columbus first brought corn back to Europe from the New World in the sixteenth century (he first encountered it in Cuba), drying and then grinding the kernels became popular as a way to retain most of the nutritive properties of corn while turning it into a nonperishable staple. The resulting cornmeal gradually replaced other grains in the making of the porridge that replaced pulmentum. Thus today's polenta truly is a direct descendant of the Romans' pulmentum. Relatively nutritious (it has significant amounts of starches, fats, and carotenes, which are converted by the body into Vitamin A), versatile, nonperishable, and affordable, it soon became ubiquitous in northern Italy. Up until the eighteenth century it was consumed almost exclusively by the lower classes, but somewhere along the way it changed into much, much more than just the meat of the poor.

By the eighteenth century, polenta was developing a cult following in the regions of Venice and Lombardy, and poets and playwrights immortalized the preparation of this once-simple food. Every middle-class Italian family had its *paiolo*, an untinned copper pot with a narrow bottom that made the polenta less likely to scorch during the long cooking time. A popular dish consisted of legions of tiny songbirds, barded with fat and spit-roasted, then perched insouciantly on a huge bed of soft polenta. Waverley Root, in his book *The Food of Italy*, described the "beady eyes [of the songbirds] fixed reproachfully on the diner, a sight which has been known to indispose Anglo-Saxons." Polenta and small birds have an affinity for one another that continues to exist to the present day.

Just days before his death in 1786, Frederick the Great of Prussia, who was a famous glutton, consumed "a meal that included polenta made with an abundance of Parmesan and with garlic squeezed over it, a large piece of beef stewed in brandy, and an eel pie that was so highly spiced that a bystander remarked that 'it must have been baked in hell'." This substantial meal was believed by many to have led to his death, but that doesn't mean polenta is bad for you—a little restraint is all that is needed. Polenta can be as bland and inexpensive or as flavorful and costly as you decide to make it.

Polenta Today

ALL OVER ITALY TODAY, FROM SIMPLE TRATTORIAS TO TEMPLES OF GASTRON-omy, polenta is consumed as a staple and as a delicacy. More often than not, it is accompanied by white truffles, rare wild mushrooms, rich cheeses, and other costly ingredients. In northern Italy families of all classes still keep a *paiolo*. Polenta is chilled, sliced, grilled or sautéed; served up as an appetizer, breakfast, dessert, main course, or side dish.

In fact, cornmeal—polenta is simply coarse yellow cornmeal—appears in the cuisine of many cultures: In the Republic of Georgia, where the corn bread is called *mchadi*, cornmeal has become such an integral part of the cuisine that when confronted with the fact that corn was first grown by the American Indians, a local Georgian said, "It only proves that those Indians were lost Georgians who somehow got to America—with corn in their pockets." In Romania, cornmeal is a staple known as *mamaliga,* which is made into a bread called *mamaliga de aur* (bread of gold). In Switzerland, cornmeal and water are cooked together until thick, then cooled, cut with a string into cubes, and fried in butter to make *riebeles.* The Greeks make a pie filled with zucchini and soft cornmeal. In South Africa, cornmeal is known as *mealie,* where it replaced millet long ago as the grain of choice for breads, puddings, and other basic kinds of nourishment. In the Caribbean islands, cornmeal and okra are cooked together to a porridgy consistency, then fried as cakes (called *fungee*) to accompany soups and stews. In fact, wherever corn has landed after its journey from the New World, the locals have made it their own.

In the American South, cornmeal is a staple too. How is polenta different from the cornmeal dishes of the South? The grain is exactly the same (though Italians usually use a coarser grind), but it is the preparation that is so different. Italian polenta often stars as the centerpiece of a meal, rather than as a side dish, and although it is sometimes made into little cakes or cookies, it is never combined with flour and baking powder and raised into a bread. It is also often sweetened for breakfast or dessert, a treatment not found in the South.

Cornmeal in one form or another has influenced and been a part of the diet of people all over the world, but it is the Italians who have elevated this simple food to the sublime. Now polenta is taking other countries by storm. In the United States the golden grain is showing up on the best menus in the country, and plenty of home cooks are following the lead. And why not? You can have it sweet or savory; hard or soft; made up with milk, broth, or wine, garlic and Parmesan; as a sandwich, filled and deep-fried; as lasagne; as a crunchy wrapping for a trout; or as a breakfast toast, studded with golden raisins and drizzled with warm maple syrup. In fact, it is as versatile, or more so, than our usual staple starches— potatoes, rice, and pasta. Like the potato, it is a canvas for the creativity and financial condition of the cook—served with butter and herbs when you are busy or pinching pennies, layered with truffles and porcini on better days.

About This Book

THERE ARE SECRETS TO SUCCESS WITH POLENTA. IN INEXPERIENCED HANDS it can become wet, flavorless, and stodgy. Discovering those secrets takes many hours of research. I have done that research for you, and even as a longtime polenta-lover, I've found a few real eye-openers, like the fact that constant, slavish stirring simply isn't required. This book reveals for the first time all the secrets and variations, and answers all your questions: "What about instant polenta—I don't have time to stir for 40 minutes?" "Can you really make polenta in a microwave? Does it save any time?" "Please, tell me how to make polenta without lumps in it!"

This is not a book about traditional Italian polenta—it is about great ideas, international flavors, and sensible innovation. Classic recipes have not been abandoned—a simple soft polenta with butter and cheese, wine-braised game hens on a bed of crisp grilled polenta, delicate polenta crostini topped with basil pesto—old friends are there alongside the new.

Give this bright yellow grain a chance in your kitchen and it will become one of your favorite staple ingredients. After all, generations of Italians couldn't be wrong!

A Polenta Primer

BOTH NEWCOMERS AND ESTABLISHED FANS of polenta may ask what is the difference between polenta and that staple of the American South, cornmeal. Grits, cornmeal, hominy, *mealie, mamaliga,* polenta—the truth is that there are few if any differences in the uncooked grain. Corn and its by-products are such a ubiquitous and versatile foodstuff that every culture has its own version. The answer is very simple: Polenta is coarsely ground yellow cornmeal.

In the South, both white and yellow, fine- and medium-grind cornmeal are used in all manner of dishes, but polenta is made only with a coarse grind. It is possible to make polenta from medium-grind cornmeal, but the texture will be less toothsome. Besides, the sunny aroma of corn is much more pronounced when using the coarse grind. The reasons for this stem from the chemical reaction that takes place when liquid is added to cornmeal and heat is applied. The starch molecules in the meal begin to swell, hydrate, and soften. When a finer grind is cooked, the starch swells too soon and the texture is gluey and bland-tasting. (If you have encountered polenta cooked incorrectly, you may have had this unpleasant experience.) In coarse-grind cornmeal, the starch molecules take much longer to hydrate and the grains are still distinct and separate when the process is finished. This is why the controversy exists as to how long polenta should be stirred. You might say, "One man's gritty mush is another's heavenly ambrosia."

Throughout this book I have called for coarsely ground yellow cornmeal, which in Italy would be labeled polenta. In America, it is usually but not always labeled polenta; it is available in every Italian grocery and most specialty food stores and can easily be ordered by mail (page 117). You can tell if the grind is coarse by examining the grains closely: The meal should be gritty, like the gray sand on a beach that isn't as fine as you'd really like for sunbathing. All the recipes in this book were tested using such a product, and I find its finished texture to be superior to any other.

You may have noticed if you've read a few polenta recipes elsewhere that the cooking and stirring times vary from as little as ten minutes to as long as one hour. Coarsely ground meal does require a longer cooking time to reach that creamy but still chewy consistency. I can only imagine that perhaps some domestic recipes used finely ground cornmeal. When it comes to cooking times, your personal taste and the recipe will dictate how long to cook the polenta. But the image of a cook tied to the stove, manhandling a long paddle stuck in a gluey mush is a fallacy. Polenta can be manipulated just like bread dough—you make it work around you, and it appreciates any time you put into it. It does not require constant stirring—once every minute or two is enough—and for grilled, sautéed, and baked shapes, it can wait for you for up to 24 hours from the time you poured it onto a surface to set.

For Hans Röckenwagner's Polenta Fries (page 102), he stirs the polenta for only five minutes before leaving it to set. It will be cooked again later, and that's why the cooking times vary throughout the book, from Hans's five minutes to the 30 minutes in the truly ultimate polenta dish (page 47), where I wanted the texture of baby food so that nothing would interfere with the star of the show—the white truffle.

In Italy, where many of the best polenta dishes have their roots, the time spent stirring is considered well worth it. Some humorists, even Julia Child, have suggested that Italian recipes call for vigorous stirring for at least an hour because it was the ideal way to get grandmother out of the way for a while and give her a reason to feel important. It is true that in the extensive testing process I've found it simply doesn't take an hour—25 to 30 minutes is plenty—so perhaps the rumor is true. But again there is also the matter of personal taste: You may find that you like the polenta with more of a bite still left in it or that you prefer it perfectly soft. If so, adjust your cooking time by a few minutes.

Several different types of cornmeal are available:

Polenta Available packaged from a French company called Croix de Savoie and from Italian companies such as Molino e Frantoio and Beretta. Available loose in bulk at Italian groceries and health-food stores. Also available by mail order (page 117).

Stone-ground cornmeal Available in some health-food stores and by mail order. This has good flavor but needs to be refrigerated so that the oils do not become rancid. Be sure to check that it is coarsely ground.

Polenta nera Literally black polenta, a 50-50 mixture of buckwheat flour and yellow cornmeal popular in the Valtellina region of northern Italy. It is often paired with polenta's traditional partners, such as game and wild mushrooms. In my opinion, this grayish porridge is not something I would want on my table. For me, the only benefit of polenta nera is the vitamins which the buckwheat adds to the dish: niacin, potassium, and phosphorus.

Instant polenta Widely available, usually packaged in a 13-ounce box, it costs about three times as much as traditional polenta. When I first started to experiment with polenta in Spain, I often used the instant variety for dishes in which the set polenta was cut into squares and grilled. After having tested and tasted the recipes in this book made with traditional polenta, though, I don't use it anymore unless I am in a real rush. It is an acceptable substitute, again a matter of personal taste.

For a simple dish like Three-Cheese Soft Polenta (page 100) or Braised Beef Short Ribs over Soft Polenta with Thyme (pages 71–72) you could certainly substitute the instant variety. Recently Beretta, which sells an excellent traditional polenta, has been exporting an instant version in a 500-gram bag. This Beretta Express has a coarser grain than the other instants, which makes it preferable for me. Simply follow the recipe as it stands, stirring the polenta for only five or six minutes instead of the longer time called for with the traditional grain.

Premade polenta A recent item, packaged in a large tube that resembles liverwurst or pork sausage. If you are in a hurry and want a simple crostini base for a mushroom ragout hors d'oeuvre (page 51) or a quickly grilled accompaniment for meat, poultry, or fish, then this is a great product, but there is no way to get additional flavor into the polenta and your shape options are limited to a three-inch diameter round. I'm glad that the fancy food producers are acknowledging the popularity of polenta by launching this product, but I hope it won't stop people from learning how much more you can do by making the polenta yourself.

Medium-ground yellow cornmeal Available under several brand names, such as Albers, Quaker Oats, and Goya. You could substitute this kind of cornmeal if you can't find the real thing, but it produces results that I can't stand behind. If you can find Goya's coarsely ground yellow cornmeal, it is quite acceptable.

Finely ground yellow cornmeal Do not use this to prepare the recipes in this book. The starch molecules break down too quickly, giving a gluey result.

Grits A dish popular in the South, made from boiling ground hominy (dried corn) in water and/or milk, with a little butter, until soft and slightly soupy but "full-bodied enough so that they don't run on the plate" (or should I say "it doesn't"—the old controversy still rages). Connoisseurs insist that the dish cook for at least an hour. Grits are served for breakfast; covered with gravies; accompanied by quail, sausages, or shrimp; and leftover grits are cut into shapes and fried. Remind you of anything?

In 1607, settlers who first came ashore at Jamestown were offered steaming bowls of *rockahominy,* which the Indians called "corn without skin." I doubt if you could find a Southerner who would agree that grits are a direct descendant of polenta, or vice versa in Italy. It is

probably fairer to say that the two dishes evolved separately but simultaneously.

The Nutritive Properties of Cornmeal

ALTHOUGH CORN IS ONE OF THE FEW COMplex carbohydrates inexpensive and plentiful enough to feed the world, it is not considered a complete food because it lacks a very important vitamin, niacin. It also lacks two of the essential amino acids, lysine and tryptophan, also present in warm milk.

Soon after corn and its by-products were first introduced to Europe as a replacement for wheat in the sixteenth century, a disease called pellagra became prevalent among the lower classes who ate only cornmeal porridge. At the time, the disease was not understood and was ascribed to various causes, from contaminated corn to the fact that the victims were weak by nature. In 1915, a U.S. government commission decided that pellagra was an infectious disease. It wasn't until the late thirties that the disease was found to result from a diet lacking in niacin. Before the arrival of cornmeal, wheat (plentiful in niacin), had provided a complete diet for the common people of southern Europe, and corn was mistakenly assumed to be equally nutritious.

Poultry, meats, and fish are good sources of niacin, as are vegetables to a lesser degree. When cornmeal is combined with dairy products such as milk, butter, and cheese, it acquires the two missing amino acids and becomes a complete food. (I often use this as an excuse to add more cheese to my polenta.) Any balanced diet will easily make up for the few nutritive deficiencies of cornmeal, and it is certainly rich in protein.

Secrets for Success

MOST ITALIAN COOKBOOKS BEGIN A POLENTA recipe with the direction "Make the polenta as usual." This may be fine for families whose cooking techniques have been honed through four or five generations of training and experimentation, but for those who are new to cooking polenta, or have been disappointed with their past attempts, there is a little more to it than that.

Equipment

FOR CENTURIES, ITALIANS USED AN unlined copper pot called a *paiolo* for making polenta. It had either a rounded bottom (this meant you couldn't put it down on the stove—torture!) or a very narrow flat base. I know of only one gourmet cookware mail-order catalogue (Sur La Table, page 117) that offers the narrow-bottomed pot, but it is expensive. Some of the better cookware manufacturers offer a classic French *sauteuse*, a pan with a base about one and one-half inches smaller than the diameter of the top (excellent for making sauces that must reduce rapidly). This makes a perfect polenta pan, as long as it is made of heavy-gauge commercial aluminum, stainless steel, or copper. The narrow base means that there is less polenta exposed to the direct heat and therefore less that could scorch or stick. If you are not ready to invest in an expensive pan before you know if you even like polenta, just use a large heavy saucepan and make sure to get your wooden paddle well into the corners when you are stirring.

As to the stirring tool, I prefer a wooden paddle because with a spoon, a lump of hard polenta often forms in the bowl of the spoon and stays there indefinitely. Flat paddles are widely available because many cooks prefer them for stirring thick sauces. Try to find a paddle with a nice long handle so that you are less likely to be burned by spattering polenta, but be sure it is thick and strong—polenta can get pretty solid and a weak handle could easily snap.

I find the best way to ensure a lump-free polenta is to begin the stirring process with a whisk and then switch to a paddle. A large, sturdy stainless steel balloon whisk is ideal for this.

Other equipment that will be helpful for preparing the recipes in this book:

❧ Various size metal roasting pans for leaving the polenta to set in recipes where it is later cut into shapes and cooked again by another method. If your pans are different sizes just use the one closest to the size called for in the recipe.

❧ A large covered cast-iron and enamel casserole, one that would comfortably hold a five-pound chicken. This is something most kitchens have anyway, and if you don't, it should be high on your list of priorities. There is really no other way to get perfect results when braising beef short ribs, veal shanks, or little game birds, or when making stews like Lamb and Artichoke Stew (pages 69–70).

Earthenware baking and ceramic soufflé dishes in various sizes are great for both cooking and presentation. In Spain I collected many terra-cotta dishes that are glazed on the inside but not on the outside, and these are now widely available in the United States.

A large piping bag with an assortment of plain and fancy tips will come in handy not only for Gorgonzola Puffs (page 60) but also for piping mashed potatoes, for filling little pastry cases with savory mousses for a cocktail party, and of course for cake decorating.

A ten-inch cast-iron skillet is a piece of equipment I went without for many years, and now that I have one I wonder how I did. Cast iron takes years to achieve perfect seasoning, but it's still very useful in the meantime.

A heavy pan or deep-fat fryer for deep-frying, and a thermometer. Food that is deep-fried at the correct temperature is never greasy—that's why I always specify bringing the temperature back up to 375°F before cooking the second and third batches of deep-fried foods.

A large springform pan. In the Cabbage-wrapped Torta (pages 58–59), I call for an 11-inch springform pan. That size was easy to find in Spain because the classic potato tortilla was often made up in one for a crowd, but you may need to search for it in America. This size pan is very useful for extra-large cheesecakes and pasta frittatas as well.

Technique

WHEN RISOTTO FIRST GAINED IN POPULARity many cooks were afraid to try cooking it at home. It was enjoyed in restaurants but thought to be too complex for even a relatively sophisticated home cook because of the timing, the nonstop stirring, and the risk of producing a bland, mushy dish if you got it wrong. Risotto, after a few expert cookbooks took the mystery out of it, has become a staple of home cooks all across the country, and polenta will, I predict, be exactly the same. There are a few rules for polenta, but they are not difficult to learn, and once you understand them the mystery will just disappear.

The main ingredient of polenta must be coarsely ground yellow cornmeal, which is often but not always labeled as polenta. Once you have measured out the polenta called for in the recipe, the next step is to bring a quantity of liquid to a simmer in a heavy saucepan, usually about four times the volume of the polenta. This could be water, and/or any combination of milk, chicken stock, or mushroom soaking liquid. Salt is added at this stage. Salt is imperative—it slows down the swelling process of the starch molecules so that the flavor has time to develop and the liquid can be evenly absorbed. I like to use coarse sea salt, but any salt is acceptable. Always use one teaspoon of coarse sea salt per cup of polenta, unless the recipe is for sweet polenta, in which case a little less is fine. If you use table salt, add a generous half-teaspoon in place of one teaspoon of coarse sea salt.

The next step is to get the polenta into the liquid without causing any lumps to form, and there are several ways to do this. I usually put the measured polenta into a glass measuring cup with a lip, then with my left hand I can pour a slow and steady stream of polenta into the simmering water, while using my right hand to stir constantly with a wire whisk. Some old— and not-so-old—cookbooks advocate grabbing a handful of polenta and letting it drizzle out from between your fingers from a great height, but I find this gets messy. The idea is to add the polenta so slowly that the liquid doesn't stop simmering. One technique that has come down to us from the old days and one that I still use is to stir all the time in the same direction (traditionally clockwise) until all the grains of polenta are absorbed by the water. There may be no scientific basis for this advice, but it certainly works. Having gotten the polenta safely into the liquid, I put down the whisk and switch to a wooden paddle. The whisk has served its purpose and wouldn't be strong enough to stir the polenta over the longer period as it begins to thicken.

Now begins the stirring, but contrary to most authorities who insist polenta must be stirred constantly without a break, I happily leave the polenta for one or two minutes between stirs while attending to some other kitchen chore. Admittedly, you can't go out to the shed and start reorganizing your gardening tools, but this technique is unlikely to tire you out unless you are ridiculously unfit. When stirring, though, be sure to 'l the way to the bottom of the pan and all around ·shing the paddle right into the corners of

the pan to involve every grain of polenta each time you stir, otherwise this technique will not work. This is when you must be very careful to avoid being splattered by bubbling hot polenta, which can cause burns on the hands, arms, and even face. It is only at the beginning, while the mixture is fairly loose, that this is a danger, and by keeping the heat very low—high heat equals spitting polenta—and using a long-handled paddle you can generally avoid this danger. It is also possible to partially cover the pan in between stirring, and stand well away from the pan as you stir.

How long to stir depends on how the polenta will eventually be served and your personal taste. If the polenta is to be cooked again later, ten to twenty minutes is enough. If the polenta is going to be served soft, 25 to 30 minutes is best. For an experiment to see how you prefer your polenta, try stirring it for a whole hour, adding a ladleful of boiling water if it gets so thick that it is impossible to stir. This is the way many Italians cook their polenta—until it is so soft that there is no texture left at all. If you like it that way, then adjust your cooking times accordingly.

Finally, black or white pepper, butter and/or Parmesan and any other flavoring ingredients are stirred in. If the polenta is to be served soft, it should be served right away, though it can be held for up to four hours. If the polenta will be cut into shapes for cooking again later, it is poured or scooped out onto a surface, spread evenly, and left to set. Traditionally the polenta was poured directly onto a marble or stone work surface, but I usually spread it in a pan so that

I can transfer it to the refrigerator to rest overnight. Depending on the consistency of the cooked polenta, spreading it evenly can be a daunting chore, but running the rubber or metal spatula under very hot running water every few seconds while spreading makes the process quite easy. Any additional water that you may add to the polenta by doing this will evaporate by the time you cook it again anyway. Traditional Italian, Romanian, and Swiss recipes all call for cutting the set polenta into shapes with a string held taut with both hands, but in fact a large knife is fine.

Microwave and Double Boiler Polenta

THESE TWO TECHNIQUES HAVE HAD THEIR advocates recently. One of them I must completely disdain, but the other is a viable option.

Microwave polenta takes marginally less time than the traditional method, and only needs to be stirred once every six minutes. That is a bonus, to be sure, but the polenta tends to be bland and tasteless for some reason, perhaps because stirring less doesn't bring out the corn flavor as much as the usual vigorous stirring. I don't recommend this method.

To make polenta in a double boiler, follow the same procedure as for polenta in a pan at the beginning, except that it all takes place in the top of a double boiler set over two inches of simmering water. Then the pan is covered and stirring is limited to once every ten to fifteen minutes, for about one hour and fifteen minutes. This may be a good option for cooks who have plenty of other things to do while they are pre-

paring the meal, but I find I am more likely to forget to stir with the longer interval than with only one or two minutes between stirs. I also don't want to be tied to the stove for such a long period of time. The results are quite good with this method, however, and it is certainly an option to explore if you don't find the traditional way of cooking polenta to your liking.

Holding Soft Polenta

ONE TIME WHEN I DO USE A DOUBLE boiler is to hold soft polenta until I am ready to serve. This is very helpful if, for instance, the menu includes a sauté that must be done at the very last minute, or if you would like to sit with your guests and enjoy the cocktail hour. Soft polenta can be held for up to four hours, covered tightly with foil and set over a pan of simmering water. You will need to stir it once every fifteen minutes or so and, if it gets too thick, add a ladleful of boiling water or stock to loosen it.

Problems

Here are a few common problems and their solutions:

PROBLEM: The polenta mixture seized up into a solid mass within moments of being stirred into the simmering liquid.

SOLUTION: *Add the polenta slowly so that the liquid never stops simmering. Do not add polenta to rapidly boiling water.*

PROBLEM: The polenta is lumpy.

SOLUTION: *Use a whisk to stir in the polenta when it is first added. Always stir in the same direction during the initial stirring time.*

PROBLEM: The polenta was bubbling so actively that it burned me with globs of hot porridge.

SOLUTION: *Keep the heat very low and stand away from the pan as you stir. Use a long-handled paddle. Keep the pan partially covered between stirring and use the cover as a shield as you begin to stir.*

PROBLEM: The polenta at the bottom of the pan was so thick that I couldn't stir it, so it scorched.

SOLUTION: *Add a ladleful of boiling water to the polenta during the stirring time if it becomes too thick to stir. Make sure you reach the paddle all the way into the corners of the pan every time you stir.*

Chicken Stock

If you have the time, it is well worth making your own stock. Save backs, wings, and other raw or cooked chicken trimmings in the freezer until you have enough ingredients and time to make up a batch of stock. Then freeze it in one- or two-cup quantities for easy thawing. If you have some ham and like the flavor, add a little. I think it gives a nice complex flavor to the stock.

MAKES ABOUT 3 QUARTS

4 pounds raw chicken backs, necks, or wings and/or leftover chicken carcasses from roasting

1 large onion, peeled and quartered

1 medium carrot, cut into 1-inch lengths

1 stalk celery, cut into 1-inch lengths

1 bay leaf

5 black peppercorns

1 sprig of parsley

1 slice smoked ham, fat removed, diced (optional)

Combine all the ingredients in a 5-quart kettle or Dutch oven, cover with water by about 1½ inches, and bring slowly to a simmer over medium heat. Skim off the foam that rises to the top during the first 10 minutes with a large, flat spoon. Simmer the stock gently for 2 hours, skimming the fat and foam occasionally. If you want the final stock to be clear, make sure that the liquid never rises above a slow simmer.

Strain the stock through a colander into a bowl and discard the solids. For a clear stock, strain again through a double thickness of slightly dampened cheesecloth. Refrigerate the stock until cold. Remove the layer of fat that rises to the top before using the stock or freezing it in smaller quantities.

Quick Chicken Stock

If you are in a hurry, you can do very well by enriching the flavor of commercial chicken stock. Start with either canned low-sodium chicken broth or one of the chicken stock base products sold for making up with boiling water. I recommend you avoid bouillon cubes.

MAKES 1 QUART

Combine all the ingredients in a large saucepan and simmer gently for 45 minutes. Strain, discarding the solids, and use as required.

1 quart canned or made-from-base
   chicken broth

1 raw chicken wing

1 small carrot, cut into 1-inch lengths

1 stalk celery, cut into 1-inch lengths

1 thick slice onion

2 black peppercorns

½ bay leaf

1 sprig of parsley if available

1 ounce smoked ham, fat removed,
   diced (optional)

Breakfast and Brunch

23   *Polenta with Poached Eggs, Smoked Salmon, and Chives*

24   *Fried Polenta Squares with Golden Raisins and Maple Syrup*

27   *Skillet Cornbread with Corn, Bacon, and Jack Cheese*

28   *Apple and Dried Cherry Fritters*

29   *Polentina with Bananas and Clover Honey*

31   *Pancakes with Blueberries and Crème Fraîche*

32   *Cinnamon Popovers (Apple Compote)*

34   *Sautéed Polenta Rounds with Prune-Kumquat Compote*

Polenta with Poached Eggs,

Smoked Salmon, and Chives

This is Sunday morning comfort food at its best. Easy to prepare, glorious to look at and eat, the fluffy yellow polenta makes a soft bed for a simple poached egg and its blanket of smoked salmon. Chives add a welcome bite. Just add a jug of freshly squeezed orange juice, perhaps a bit of champagne, and linen napkins and you've created the ultimate breakfast. · SERVES 6

TO MAKE THE POLENTA: Preheat the oven to 325°F. Butter a 2-quart casserole or soufflé dish.

IN A LARGE SAUCEPAN bring the milk to a boil and add the salt, butter, and sugar. Reduce the heat and, when the liquid is simmering, sprinkle the polenta evenly over it in a very slow, thin stream, whisking constantly in the same direction until all the grains have been incorporated and no lumps remain. Switch to a wooden paddle and stir every 1 to 2 minutes for 10 to 15 minutes, or until the mixture pulls away from the sides of the pan and the grains of polenta have begun to soften. Remove from the heat. Add the yolks, buttermilk, and baking powder and stir to mix.

IN A CLEAN BOWL, beat the egg whites to stiff peaks. Gently fold into the polenta mixture. Scoop into the prepared baking dish.

BAKE FOR 40 TO 45 MINUTES, or until a skewer inserted into the center comes out clean. The center should still jiggle a little when shaken.

ABOUT 10 MINUTES before the polenta will be done, in a large sauté pan with high sides and a tight-fitting lid, bring a generous amount of water to a rolling boil. Turn off the heat and immediately break the eggs gently just above the surface of the water. Cover the pan and leave undisturbed for about 3 minutes if you like the yolk runny, 5 minutes if you like a set yolk. With a slotted spoon, remove the poached eggs to a plate lined with a paper towel to drain briefly.

SPOON SOME OF THE SOFT POLENTA into each of 6 shallow heated breakfast bowls and make a well in the center. Spoon a poached egg into each well, then cover with a slice of smoked salmon. Sprinkle with some of the chives and serve immediately.

2 cups milk

1 teaspoon coarse sea salt

2 tablespoons unsalted butter

2 teaspoons sugar

3/4 cup polenta or coarsely ground yellow cornmeal

3 large, fresh eggs, separated, at room temperature, yolks lightly beaten

3/4 cup buttermilk

1 teaspoon baking powder

6 large eggs, free-range if available

6 slices smoked salmon (about 1/4 pound)

10 chives, cut into 1-inch lengths

Fried Polenta Squares

with Golden Raisins and Maple Syrup

These raisin-studded squares are made especially for breakfast, and with their faint aroma of cinnamon and sugary crust, they make a stupendous winter-morning treat.

SERVES 6

2 cups milk

1 cup water

1 teaspoon coarse sea salt

1 teaspoon sugar

1 cup polenta or coarsely ground
  yellow cornmeal

3 tablespoons golden raisins

1/4 teaspoon ground cinnamon

2 tablespoons unsalted butter

1 teaspoon canola or vegetable oil

1 cup pure maple syrup, or to taste

1 teaspoon confectioners' sugar

IN A MEDIUM-SIZE HEAVY SAUCEPAN, combine the milk, water, salt, and sugar and bring the mixture to a boil. Reduce the heat and sprinkle in the polenta in a very slow, thin stream, whisking in the same direction until all the grains have been incorporated and no lumps remain. Reduce the heat to very low. Switch to a wooden paddle and stir well once every 1 or 2 minutes for 15 to 20 minutes, or until the mixture comes away from the sides of the pan and the grains of polenta have begun to soften. Stir in the raisins and the cinnamon. The mixture should be so thick that the paddle will stand upright for 3 seconds.

RINSE AN 8 x 12-INCH PAN with cold water and shake it dry. Mound the polenta into the pan and, using a spatula repeatedly dipped in very hot water, spread the polenta into an even layer just under 1/2 inch thick. Cover with a tea towel and let rest for at least 1 hour at room temperature or up to 24 hours in the refrigerator. Cut the polenta into six 4-inch squares.

IN A LARGE HEAVY SAUTÉ PAN, heat the butter and oil over medium-low heat. In 2 batches, fry the polenta slices for 4 minutes on 1 side, then turn to the other side and fry until golden, another 3 to 4 minutes. Keep the first batch warm in a low oven while you fry the remaining squares, adding a little more butter to the pan if necessary.

MEANWHILE, heat the maple syrup in a glass pitcher set inside a small pan of cold water. Or heat in a microwave.

SPRINKLE a little confectioners' sugar around the edges of 6 warmed breakfast plates, place a polenta square in the center of each, and drizzle with about 1 tablespoon of the syrup. Serve immediately, passing the remaining syrup at the table.

Skillet Cornbread with Corn, Bacon, and Jack Cheese

Sometimes a substantial breakfast is called for—after an early-morning fishing expedition in which no fish were caught, for example, or before a particularly arduous home-improvement job. This is a California-style presentation using polenta in a very American way—Italians never make their cornmeal into bread, but we certainly do, and since this book is for people everywhere who love good food, why not include it here?

SERVES 6

PLACE 1 TABLESPOON of the melted butter in a well-seasoned 10-inch cast-iron skillet and place in a cold oven. Heat the oven to 375°F.

IN A MEDIUM SAUCEPAN, bring the milk to a boil over medium-high heat and add the salt. Reduce the heat so that the milk is simmering and sprinkle the polenta over it in a slow, thin stream, whisking constantly in the same direction until it is all absorbed and smooth. Remove the pan from the heat and stir in the remaining 2 tablespoons of melted butter, the buttermilk, baking powder, baking soda, corn kernels, bacon, and cheese. Stir in the egg yolks.

IN A MEDIUM MIXING BOWL, beat the egg whites until stiff. Stir ¼ of the egg whites thoroughly into the mixture to lighten it, then fold in the remaining whites, making sure not to overmix.

SWIRL THE HOT SKILLET to coat the bottom and sides evenly with the butter, then turn the mixture into the skillet and return to the oven to cook for 25 minutes, or until the center is firm. Serve with a large spoon, sprinkling a few chives over each serving.

3 tablespoons melted butter or bacon fat

2½ cups milk

½ teaspoon coarse sea salt

1¼ cups polenta or coarsely ground yellow cornmeal

1¼ cups buttermilk

1 teaspoon baking powder

½ teaspoon baking soda

1 cup fresh or thawed frozen corn kernels

8 slices of bacon, cut into ½-inch strips and cooked until crisp, then drained

6 ounces jack cheese, cut into ½-inch cubes

2 large eggs, separated, at room temperature

2 tablespoons finely chopped chives or scallion greens, for garnish

diced green peppers

polenta:
Basil & Garlic
put in Vitamix to make smooth

27

Apple and Dried Cherry
Fritters

These crusty fritters would make the perfect breakfast partner for a simple fruit salad of melon and berries, mixed exotic juices, and a fruit tea. For me, the only requirement for a breakfast dish is that it be extra simple, and this is.

SERVES 6 TO 8 AS PART OF A LARGER BREAKFAST

½ cup water

½ cup milk

1 teaspoon sugar

½ teaspoon coarse sea salt

½ teaspoon ground cloves

8 tablespoons (1 stick) unsalted
   butter

¾ cup all-purpose flour

⅓ cup polenta or coarsely ground
   yellow cornmeal

3 large eggs

1 Granny Smith apple, peeled, cored,
   and cut into ½-inch cubes

¼ cup dried cherries, coarsely
   chopped

Vegetable oil, for deep-frying

1 tablespoon confectioners' sugar

IN A LARGE HEAVY SAUCEPAN, heat the water, milk, sugar, salt, cloves, and butter over medium heat. When the butter has just melted, remove from the heat and whisk in the flour and polenta, continuing to whisk until the mixture is evenly thickened and lump free. Switching to a wooden spoon, add the eggs, one at a time, stirring well between each addition. Stir in the apple and cherries. The mixture will be quite thick.

IN A LARGE HEAVY SAUTÉ PAN with high sides or a deep-fat fryer, heat about 1½ inches of oil to 375°F. Drop large tablespoonfuls of the fritter batter, about 6 at a time, into the hot oil and fry, turning gently with tongs, for about 2 minutes on each side, or until puffed and golden brown. Transfer to a paper towel–lined plate. Keep the fritters warm in a low oven while you use up the remaining batter. Be sure to bring the oil temperature back up to 375°F before cooking each batch.

PUT THE CONFECTIONERS' SUGAR into a small strainer and sprinkle an even coating over the fritters just before serving.

NOTE: The fritters will get soggy if allowed to wait in the oven for more than a few minutes, so work quickly and serve as soon as they are all cooked.

Polentina with Bananas and Clover Honey

This is the simplest of recipes, in fact it hardly needs to be written down!
Polentina has been an early-morning staple in Italy for generations, just as its twin, cornmeal mush, is a popular
breakfast in the American South. Any ripe, soft fruit in season could be substituted for the bananas, and if you have
no diet restrictions, drizzle a little melted butter over each bowl of porridge just before serving.

SERVES 6

IN A LARGE HEAVY SAUCEPAN, bring the water, milk, salt, and sugar to a boil over medium-high heat. Reduce the heat and, when the liquid is simmering, drizzle the polenta over in a slow, thin stream, whisking constantly in the same direction until all the grains have been absorbed and the mixture is lump free. Reduce the heat to very low. Switch to a wooden paddle and stir thoroughly every 1 or 2 minutes for 15 to 30 minutes, depending on how soft you want the polenta to be. Add a little more water or milk if it gets too stiff—this should be a very liquid mixture.

WHEN THE POLENTINA IS DONE to your liking, ladle it into warm breakfast bowls, distribute the bananas over the top and drizzle with honey and melted butter, if desired.

NOTE: To make the honey easier to pour, remove the lid and place the jar in a small saucepan of cold water over medium-low heat. Warm until the water is just simmering. Remove from the heat and use an oven glove to hold the jar while you spoon some honey over each serving. Or warm the open jar of honey in the microwave for a few seconds.

2½ cups water

2½ cups regular or lowfat milk

½ teaspoon coarse sea salt

2 tablespoons sugar

1 cup polenta or coarsely ground
   yellow cornmeal

2 ripe bananas, sliced ¼ inch thick

½ cup honey

Melted butter, for drizzling (optional)

Pancakes

with Blueberries and Crème Fraîche

The blue and gold of these pancakes reminds me of spring on the central coast of California. When I was little, we spent all our vacations at a big cattle ranch north of Santa Barbara, and most of the grownups would go fishing at about 5:30 A.M. Kids, being so noisy they scared away the fish, weren't allowed to go, so we stayed behind and helped whip up something to accompany the outrageously succulent fried trout, minutes out of a stream, that we'd be breakfasting on by about 9 A.M. This is a variation on one of the fisherman's favorites. If you have a sweet-tooth you could drizzle a little warm boysenberry syrup over the top of the crème fraîche. SERVES 6

IN A MEDIUM MIXING BOWL, sift together the flour, sugar, salt, baking powder, and baking soda. Sprinkle the polenta over the other dry ingredients and toss until evenly mixed.

IN A SEPARATE BOWL, beat the eggs lightly with a fork, then add the buttermilk and the melted butter and whisk together briefly. Add the wet ingredients to the dry ingredients and mix until just blended–the batter will be a little lumpy. Gently fold in the blueberries until they are evenly distributed in the batter.

HEAT A LARGE CAST-IRON SKILLET or a griddle until it's so hot that droplets of water dance across the surface, then brush it with vegetable oil. Using a 1/4-cup measure or a 2-ounce ladle, pour the batter onto the pan or griddle and cook until large bubbles form on the top of the pancake and the edges begin to brown. Flip to the other side and cook for another minute or so, until the bottom is browned. Transfer to a paper towel–lined plate and keep warm in a low oven while you cook the remaining pancakes. Brush the pan or griddle with more vegetable oil as necessary as you cook the remaining batches.

SERVE THE PANCAKES WARM with a dollop of crème fraîche on top.

½ cup all-purpose flour

2 tablespoons sugar

½ teaspoon coarse sea salt

1 teaspoon baking powder

½ teaspoon baking soda

½ cup polenta or coarsely ground
   yellow cornmeal

2 large eggs

1 cup buttermilk

2 tablespoons unsalted butter, melted

1 cup blueberries

Vegetable oil, for brushing the griddle

½ cup crème fraîche

Cinnamon Popovers

*There is virtually no difference between a popover and a Yorkshire pudding,
the ubiquitous accompaniment to roast beef throughout the British Isles. There are, however, many variations on the
theme, and this one combines the unexpected crunch of polenta with the aroma of cinnamon, a smell that seems to shout
"Breakfast!" For a quick morning preparation, the batter may be made up the night before. All else that's needed is
coffee, juice, and perhaps a warm apple compote.* SERVES 8 TO 12

4 large eggs

1 cup and 2 tablespoons all-purpose
  flour

¼ cup polenta or coarsely ground
  yellow cornmeal

¼ teaspoon coarse sea salt

Small pinch of white pepper

¼ teaspoon ground cinnamon

1 cup and 2 tablespoons milk or
  half milk and half water

2 tablespoons unsalted butter, melted

Whipped butter and fruit preserves,
  for garnish (optional)

Apple Compote (recipe follows)
  (optional)

APPLE COMPOTE

2 Granny Smith apples

Zest of ½ lemon

1 teaspoon fresh lemon juice

1 cup unfiltered apple juice, or
  more as needed

Sugar as needed

IN A BLENDER, combine the eggs, flour, polenta, salt, pepper, and cinnamon and blend briefly. Slowly add the milk and blend until completely smooth. Cover the blender and let it rest in the refrigerator for at least 1 hour or overnight.

PLACE ½ TEASPOON of the melted butter in the bottom of each cup of a 12-cup nonstick muffin or popover pan. If you are not using a nonstick pan, spray or brush the muffin cups with vegetable oil before adding the butter. Place the pan in a cold oven and heat it to 400°F.

WHEN THE FAT IS VERY HOT (take care that the butter doesn't brown), return the blender to its base and blend again briefly. Pour an equal amount of the batter into each cup, filling each one halfway.

BAKE FOR 30 TO 35 MINUTES, or until the popovers are well risen and golden. Do not open the oven door during the first 20 minutes of the cooking time or the popovers may fall.

SERVE HOT, accompanied by butter and preserves, if desired, or apple compote, if desired.

NOTE: For savory popovers, omit the cinnamon and substitute an equal quantity of paprika.

APPLE COMPOTE: Peel and core the apples and cut them into ½-inch chunks. In a medium saucepan, combine the apples with the lemon zest, lemon juice, and enough apple juice to barely cover them. Simmer for 10 minutes, or until the apples are tender. Add sugar to taste, if desired, and stir over the heat until the sugar has dissolved. Serve warm.

Sautéed Polenta Rounds

with Prune-Kumquat Compote

This is essentially a very simple breakfast dish. All the work can be done the night before, leaving only the reheating of the compote and the sautéing of the polenta rounds for the next morning.

SERVES 6 TO 8

PRUNE-KUMQUAT COMPOTE

1 cup dried prunes (6 ounces)

1 tablespoon honey

½ cup fresh orange juice

6 kumquats, sliced into thin rounds
    and seeds removed

1 tablespoon Cointreau (optional)

POLENTA ROUNDS

2 cups milk

1 cup water

½ teaspoon coarse sea salt

1 tablespoon sugar

1 cup polenta or coarsely ground
    yellow cornmeal

2 tablespoons unsalted butter

1 teaspoon canola or vegetable oil

TO MAKE THE COMPOTE: Cover the prunes with cold water in a medium saucepan and leave them to soak for 4 hours or overnight. Bring the water to a simmer over medium-high heat and simmer for 10 minutes, or until the prunes are plump and tender. Strain them, reserving the cooking liquid, and remove the stones. Set aside.

IN A SMALL SAUCEPAN, combine the honey, ½ cup of the prune cooking liquid, and the orange juice, and bring to a boil. Reduce the heat and add the kumquats. Simmer gently for 5 to 7 minutes, or until almost tender. Remove from the heat, add the prunes, and stir to mix, adding the Cointreau, if desired. Cover and set aside while you make the polenta. (The compote may be refrigerated overnight and reheated before serving.)

TO MAKE THE POLENTA: In a medium-size heavy saucepan, combine the milk, water, salt, and sugar and bring the mixture to a boil. Reduce the heat and, when the liquid is simmering, sprinkle in the polenta in a very slow, thin stream, whisking constantly in the same direction until all the grains have been incorporated and no lumps remain. Reduce the heat to very low. Switch to a wooden paddle and stir well every 1 or 2 minutes for 15 to 20 minutes, or until the mixture comes away from the sides of the pan and the grains of polenta have begun to soften. The mixture should be so thick that the paddle will stand upright for 2 or 3 seconds.

RINSE AN 8 x 12-INCH ROASTING PAN with cold water and shake it dry. Mound the polenta in the pan and, using a spatula repeatedly dipped in very hot water, spread the polenta into an even layer just under ½ inch thick. Cover with a tea towel and let rest for at least 1 hour at room temperature or up to 24 hours in the refrigerator. Cut the polenta into eight 3-inch rounds using a biscuit cutter or the top of a glass.

WHEN READY TO SERVE, in a large heavy sauté pan, heat the butter and oil over medium-low heat. In 2 or 3 batches, fry the polenta rounds for 5 minutes on 1 side, regulating the heat so that the butter sizzles and browns but does not burn, then turn to the other side and fry until golden, 3 to 4 minutes more. Keep the first batch warm in a low oven while you fry the remaining rounds, adding a little more butter or oil to the pan as necessary.

GENTLY REHEAT THE COMPOTE until it is just warmed through. Place a polenta round or two on each warmed breakfast plate and top with a spoonful of the warm compote.

First Courses and
Hors d'Oeuvres

37   *Rosemary-Olive Pizzettas with Prosciutto*

40   *Crabmeat Polenta with Lemon and Chive Sauce*

41   *Baked Polenta with Eggplant, Sun-dried Tomatoes, and Basil Sauce*

44   *Baby Greens with Blood Oranges and Sage-Prosciutto Polenta Croutons*

47   *Soft Polenta with White Truffles and Crème Fraîche*

48   *Grilled Polenta Crostini with Smoked Trout and Mascarpone*

51   *Wild Mushroom Ragout*

52   *Deep-fried Polenta Sandwiches with Spinach and Gorgonzola*

54   *Polenta with Shiitake Mushrooms, Mascarpone, and Salmon Roe*

55   *Lentils and Greens in Broth with Polenta Croutons*

58   *Cabbage-wrapped Torta with Leeks and Pancetta*

60   *Gorgonzola Puffs*

Rosemary-Olive Pizzettas

with Prosciutto

*Making your own pizza dough is worth it, particularly when you are adding
extra-special flavors like polenta and rosemary. You'll find you can make the dough work around your schedule, not
you around it. For instance, after the little dough disks are set on the baking sheet, they can be held in the refrigerator
for up to five hours. If they have begun to rise in the fridge, just press them down with your fingertips before topping
and baking, otherwise the pizzettas will be too bready.*   SERVES 6 TO 8

TO MAKE THE DOUGH: In a glass measuring cup with a lip, combine the
water and the sugar and stir to mix. Sprinkle the yeast over the top and
allow to stand for 10 minutes until it has a frothy head. If no frothy head
forms, the yeast is bad and you will need to start again.

IN THE BOWL OF A FOOD PROCESSOR fitted with the metal blade, combine the all-purpose flour with the polenta, whole wheat flour, rosemary,
olive oil, and salt. Process briefly just to blend. With the motor running,
pour the yeast mixture steadily through the feed tube and process until
the mixture forms a rough ball on the central stem. If the dough has not
formed a ball within 20 seconds, remove the cover and sprinkle a tablespoon of water over the dough, then process again. The dough should be
processed for a total time of about 45 seconds. Replace the feed tube
cover so that no air will get in, and leave the dough in the processor to
rise for 1 to 1½ hours, or until it has doubled, puffed, and softened.

WHILE THE DOUGH IS RISING, soak the porcini mushrooms in 1 cup of
very hot water for 30 minutes.

TO MAKE THE TOPPING: About 45 minutes before the dough will be
ready, heat the oil in a medium skillet over low heat. Add the onion and
prosciutto and cook slowly for 20 to 25 minutes, or until very soft and
slightly caramelized. Drain the porcinis and squeeze them as dry as
possible. Chop them coarsely, then add to the pan. Add the thyme and

PIZZA DOUGH

⅔ cup warm water (about 110°F)

½ teaspoon sugar

1 teaspoon active dry yeast

2 cups all-purpose flour

½ cup polenta or coarsely ground
   yellow cornmeal

2 tablespoons whole wheat flour

1 tablespoon finely chopped fresh
   rosemary or 1 teaspoon dried
   rosemary

2 tablespoons extra virgin olive oil

1 teaspoon coarse sea salt

PIZZA TOPPING

½ ounce dried porcini mushrooms

2 tablespoons extra virgin olive oil

2 medium-size sweet onions, coarsely
   chopped

3 ounces thinly sliced prosciutto,
   coarsely chopped

(cont.)

2 teaspoons finely chopped fresh
  thyme, or 1 teaspoon dried thyme,
  crumbled
8 Italian oil-cured black olives, pitted
  and coarsely chopped
4 ounces smoked mozzarella, sliced
  and torn into small pieces

stir to mix, then remove the pan from the heat. (The mixture may be cooled and refrigerated for up to 2 hours. It does not need to be reheated before topping the pizza.)

PREHEAT THE OVEN to 450°F.

PROCESS THE DOUGH in the food processor again for 5 seconds, then turn it out onto a lightly floured board. Work the dough together and form into 8 to 10 equal-size balls. Place the dough balls on a lightly oiled large baking sheet, cover with a slightly dampened towel, and allow to rest for 15 minutes. Press each ball out into a 3-inch round. Poke the olives into the tops of the pizzettas. Mound an equal amount of the onion-prosciutto mixture on each one, leaving a 1/4-inch border. Divide the mozzarella among the pizzettas.

BAKE FOR 10 TO 12 MINUTES, or until the edges are golden and the cheese has melted. Serve immediately.

Crabmeat Polenta with Lemon and Chive Sauce

This is a dish that is unquestionably Californian in style—an Italian grand-mother might raise her eyebrows, but it speaks to me vividly of Sunday brunch in the garden.   SERVES 6

LEMON AND CHIVE SAUCE

1 cup sour cream

1 tablespoon vermouth

1 tablespoon fresh lemon juice

2 tablespoons finely chopped parsley

1 tablespoon finely snipped chives

Salt and freshly ground white pepper

CRABMEAT POLENTA

2 tablespoons extra virgin olive oil

2 medium shallots, finely chopped

1 clove garlic, minced

2 cups milk

3 cups chicken or mild fish stock

1 teaspoon coarse sea salt

1 cup polenta or coarsely ground
    yellow cornmeal

Freshly ground pepper

2 large eggs, separated

¾ cup freshly grated Parmesan

2 plum tomatoes, peeled, seeded,
    and diced

15 oil-cured black olives, pitted and
    quartered

4 scallions, white parts only, sliced

6 ounces fresh lump crabmeat,
    shredded into large chunks

TO MAKE THE SAUCE: Combine all the ingredients in a bowl and stir together. Cover and chill until needed.

TO MAKE THE POLENTA: Preheat the oven to 425°F. Butter a 7 x 12-inch ceramic or earthenware baking dish and set aside.

IN A LARGE HEAVY SAUCEPAN, heat the olive oil over medium-low heat. Add the shallots and garlic and sauté, stirring occasionally, for 4 to 5 minutes or until translucent. Add the milk, chicken stock, and salt to the pan and increase the heat to medium-high. When the liquid is simmering, gradually sprinkle the polenta over in a very slow, thin stream, whisking constantly in the same direction until no lumps remain. Reduce the heat to low. Switch to a wooden paddle and stir every 1 or 2 minutes for 15 to 20 minutes, or until the mixture pulls away from the sides of the pan and the grains of polenta have begun to soften. It will be quite a loose mixture. Remove from the heat. Stir in the pepper, egg yolks, ¼ cup of the Parmesan, the diced tomatoes, olives, and scallions until thoroughly blended.

IN A MIXING BOWL, beat the egg whites to stiff peaks. Stir a quarter of the whites thoroughly into the polenta mixture to lighten it, then gently fold in the remaining whites, taking care not to over-fold. Very gently fold in the crabmeat, using as few strokes as possible. Spoon the polenta into the prepared dish, smoothing the top with a spatula. Sprinkle the remaining ½ cup Parmesan evenly over the top.

BAKE FOR 25 TO 30 MINUTES, or until the polenta pulls away from the sides of the baking dish and the center is firm and golden. Let cool for 5 minutes. Spoon onto heated plates and serve immediately, passing the sauce separately.

Baked Polenta

with Eggplant, Sun-dried Tomatoes, and Basil Sauce

For this dish, the polenta can be made up to 24 hours ahead of time, or the whole dish can be assembled and held for a few hours before cooking. The first time I made this was for a summer afternoon barbecue at my stepmother Elizabeth's temporary home in the Pacific Palisades. The tomatoes and the basil came from my garden, her terrace was warm and filled with flowers, and we drank a grassy Honig Sauvignon Blanc that perfectly balanced the slight acidity of the tomatoes. SERVES 6

IN A LARGE HEAVY SAUCEPAN, heat the oil over medium heat. Add the onion and garlic and sauté, stirring occasionally, for 5 to 6 minutes or until softened. Add the chicken stock, milk, and salt and increase the heat to high. When the liquid is simmering, gradually sprinkle the polenta over in a slow, thin stream, whisking constantly in the same direction until all the grains are incorporated and no lumps remain. Reduce the heat to very low. Switch to a wooden paddle and stir every 1 or 2 minutes for 25 to 30 minutes, or until the mixture pulls away from the side of the pan and the grains of polenta have softened. Stir in the pepper and Parmesan.

RINSE AN 8 x 12-INCH PAN with cold water and shake dry. Pour the polenta into the pan and, using a rubber spatula repeatedly dipped in very hot water, spread the polenta evenly in the pan until it is just under ½ inch thick. Cover with a tea towel and allow to rest for 1 hour at room temperature or up to 24 hours in the refrigerator.

PREHEAT THE OVEN to 400°F.

TO MAKE THE SAUCE: In a medium roasting pan, bake the eggplant for 1 hour, or until tender. When cool enough to handle, peel the eggplant and cut it into ½-inch cubes; set aside. In a large heavy skillet, heat the oil over medium heat. Add the onion and sauté, stirring occasionally, for 4 to 5 minutes, or until just softened. Add the fresh tomatoes and the sun-dried tomatoes and cook, partially covered, for about 20 minutes, or until

2 tablespoons olive oil

½ cup finely chopped onion

2 cloves garlic, minced

3 cups chicken stock, preferably homemade (pages 20–21)

1 cup milk

1 teaspoon coarse sea salt

1 cup polenta or coarsely ground yellow cornmeal

¼ teaspoon white pepper

⅓ cup freshly grated Parmesan

EGGPLANT SAUCE

1 eggplant (about 1 pound), pricked in several places with a fork

2 tablespoons extra virgin olive oil

½ medium-size sweet onion, such as Maui or Walla Walla, coarsely chopped

6 medium-size ripe plum tomatoes (about 1 pound), peeled, seeded, and diced

(cont.)

thickened. Remove from the heat and add the salt, pepper, eggplant, and basil. Stir to mix. (The mixture may be cooled and refrigerated for up to 2 hours, if desired.)

WHEN READY TO SERVE, preheat the oven to 375°F. Brush an 8-inch square or 8 x 12-inch rectangular baking dish with a little olive oil.

CUT THE POLENTA into 3-inch squares and place them in the baking dish, overlapping slightly, in 2 rows. Spoon some of the sauce down either side and in the center, not covering the polenta completely. Sprinkle the feta over the exposed polenta and cover with aluminum foil.

BAKE FOR 40 TO 45 MINUTES, or until the polenta is slightly golden and the sauce is bubbling. Garnish with sprigs of fresh basil and serve immediately.

3 oil-packed sun-dried tomatoes, finely diced
½ teaspoon coarse sea salt
¼ teaspoon freshly ground black pepper
¼ cup (firmly packed) fresh basil leaves, cut into julienne

½ cup crumbled feta
Sprigs of fresh basil, for garnish

Baby Greens

with Blood Oranges and Sage-Prosciutto Polenta Croutons

When I arrived back in America after years of living in Spain, my choice of where to live was based on the availability of baby salad greens (prewashed and premixed—after years of nothing but romaine it was heaven!). Now these delicate greens are widely available and make the creation of delectable salads a much easier proposition. I wanted something tart to offset the richness of the polenta, and blood oranges were the perfect choice. SERVES 6 TO 8

SAGE-PROSCIUTTO CROUTONS

2 teaspoons extra virgin olive oil

1 ounce prosciutto, finely diced

2 cloves garlic, minced

7 fresh sage leaves, finely chopped

1 cup chicken stock, preferably homemade (pages 20-21)

1 cup water

½ teaspoon coarse sea salt

½ cup polenta or coarsely ground yellow cornmeal

Freshly ground black pepper

3 tablespoons freshly grated Parmesan

2 tablespoons butter

⅓ cup canola or vegetable oil, for frying

TO MAKE THE CROUTONS: In a large heavy saucepan heat the olive oil over medium-low heat. Add the prosciutto, garlic, and sage and sauté, stirring occasionally, until the prosciutto is crisp and the garlic is softened, about 4 minutes. Do not let the garlic burn. Transfer the mixture to a bowl and set aside.

WIPE THE INSIDE OF THE PAN with a paper towel and return to the heat. Immediately add the chicken stock, water, and salt and bring to a simmer over medium-high heat. When the liquid is simmering, gradually sprinkle the polenta over in a very slow, thin stream, whisking constantly in the same direction until all the grains have been incorporated and no lumps remain. Reduce the heat to low. Switch to a wooden paddle and stir every 1 or 2 minutes for 25 to 30 minutes, or until the mixture pulls away from the sides of the pan and the grains of polenta have softened. Add the prosciutto mixture and pepper to taste. Add the Parmesan and butter, stirring to mix evenly. The mixture will be very thick.

RINSE AN 8 X 12-INCH PAN with cold water and shake dry. Mound the polenta in the pan and, using a rubber spatula repeatedly dipped in very hot water, spread the polenta evenly in the pan until it is just under ½ inch thick. Cover with a tea towel and allow to rest for 1 hour at room temperature, or up to 24 hours in the refrigerator.

(cont.)

SALAD

5 cups (loosely packed) baby greens
   (mesclun), or a mixture of lamb's
   lettuce (mâche), radicchio, curly
   endive (frisée), and butter lettuce
2 blood oranges, rind and pith
   removed and cut into segments
3 tablespoons best-quality extra virgin
   olive oil
½ teaspoon coarse sea salt
Freshly ground black pepper
1 tablespoon aged raspberry vinegar
   (or nice white wine vinegar)

CUT THE POLENTA into approximately 1-inch squares. Heat the canola oil in a heavy skillet. In two batches if necessary, fry the croutons, nudging occasionally with a spatula to keep them separate, for 8 to 10 minutes, turning once, or until crispy and golden at the edges. With a skimmer, remove the croutons to a paper towel–lined plate and keep warm in a low oven while you fry the rest and prepare the salad.

TO PREPARE THE SALAD: In a large bowl, mound the baby greens and distribute the blood orange segments over the top. Drizzle the olive oil over the salad and toss gently until the leaves are well coated. Sprinkle on the salt, pepper to taste, and vinegar and toss again briefly to distribute the vinegar evenly. Mound an equal amount of salad on each of 6 or 8 side plates and distribute the warm croutons around the edges of the plates. Serve immediately.

Soft Polenta with White Truffles

and Crème Fraîche

I call this the ultimate polenta dish. If you can find the elusive and expensive white truffle—perhaps you have a friend returning from Milan or an ultra-premium grocer who likes you—invite your very closest friend to share it with you. Black truffles are more widely available. If you want to substitute one, paper-thin slices should be simmered for five minutes in a cup of white wine before using (save the wine for a sauce). White truffles are never cooked, just warmed, as cooking would destroy their delicate flavor. Canned truffles contain only a small hint of the flavor that surrounds, precedes, and follows the authentic fresh fungus, and should only be used in cases of dire emergency.

SERVES 2

WITH A SOFT BRUSH, clean the wrinkled skin of the truffle of any loose dirt, then wipe it with a damp cloth. With a sharp vegetable peeler, shave the truffle into a little dish. Shave 6 to 8 large curls of Parmigiano-Reggiano from the wedge into another dish. Cover and refrigerate both dishes.

HAVE 2 BEAUTIFUL SHALLOW SOUP BOWLS warming in a low oven. In a heavy saucepan, bring the water and stock to a boil and add the salt. Reduce the heat and, when the liquid is simmering, sprinkle the polenta evenly over in a very slow, thin stream, whisking constantly in the same direction until all the grains have been incorporated and no lumps remain. Reduce the heat to very low. Switch to a wooden paddle and stir every 1 or 2 minutes for about 30 minutes, or until the mixture pulls away from the sides of the pan and the grains of polenta have softened. Remove from the heat and stir in the butter and crème fraîche until they are completely incorporated.

IMMEDIATELY MOUND THE POLENTA into the heated bowls, scatter with the shaved truffle and the cheese. Return to the warm oven for 2 minutes to melt the cheese and release the aroma of the truffle. Serve immediately, stirring the truffle and cheese into the polenta before taking the first bite.

1 white truffle (½ ounce)

Wedge of aged imported
  Parmigiano-Reggiano

1 cup water

1½ cups chicken stock, preferably
  homemade (pages 20–21)

Small pinch coarse sea salt

½ cup polenta or coarsely
  ground yellow cornmeal

1 tablespoon unsalted butter

¼ cup crème fraîche

Grilled Polenta Crostini

with Smoked Trout and Mascarpone

This is a master recipe. Not only is it masterfully good but it can be used as the model for literally hundreds of crostini with different toppings. It is the ideal cocktail hour finger food. Virtually anything you like can be used as a topping, even salsa—after all, polenta is not just Italian anymore! SERVES 6 TO 8

2 cups chicken stock, preferably
   homemade (pages 20–21)

1 cup milk

1 teaspoon coarse sea salt

1 cup polenta or coarsely ground
   yellow cornmeal

4 tablespoons (½ stick) unsalted
   butter

⅓ cup freshly grated Parmesan

Freshly ground black pepper

6 ounces mascarpone (see Note)

4 ounces smoked trout, skin and
   bones removed, cut into small
   pieces

1 tablespoon finely chopped chives

IN A MEDIUM-SIZE HEAVY SAUCEPAN, combine the stock, milk, and salt and bring the mixture to a boil. Reduce the heat so that the liquid is simmering and sprinkle the polenta over it in a very slow, thin stream, whisking constantly in the same direction until all the grains have been incorporated and no lumps remain. Reduce the heat to very low. Switch to a wooden paddle and stir every 1 or 2 minutes for 15 to 20 minutes, or until the mixture comes away from the sides of the pan and the grains of polenta have begun to soften. The mixture should be so thick that the paddle will stand upright for 2 or 3 seconds. Add 2 tablespoons of the butter and the Parmesan, stirring until they are evenly distributed. Remove from the heat.

RINSE AN 8 x 12-INCH PAN with cold water and shake it dry. Mound the polenta in the pan and, using a spatula repeatedly dipped in very hot water, spread the polenta into an even layer just under ½ inch thick. Cover with a tea towel and let rest for at least 1 hour at room temperature and up to 24 hours in the refrigerator.

WHEN READY TO SERVE, preheat an indoor broiler or an outdoor grill to high heat.

MELT THE REMAINING 2 TABLESPOONS butter. Cut the polenta into twelve 2-inch squares, brush evenly with the melted butter and sprinkle with black pepper to taste. Grill about 3 inches from the heat for 5 minutes on each side, or until browned. Remove from the heat, drain

(cont.)

briefly on paper towels, if desired, and top each square with a small dollop of mascarpone, a little piece of smoked trout, and a few chives. Serve immediately.

NOTE: Mascarpone is available in Italian groceries and specialty gourmet markets. Crème fraîche could be substituted.

TOPPING VARIATIONS

- Dollops of mascarpone topped with shavings of white truffle instead of smoked trout.
- Peeled, seeded, and chopped plum tomatoes mixed with minced garlic and fresh basil, bound with olive oil, and seasoned with salt and pepper.
- Dollops of basil, parsley, or cilantro pesto.
- Slivers of Italian fontina cheese. Return the crostini to the grill until the cheese just melts, then garnish with tiny strips of prosciutto.
- Slivers of smoked mozzarella. Return the crostini to the grill until the cheese just melts, then garnish with julienned fresh basil leaves.
- Crumbled feta, topped with strips of Oven-roasted Tomatoes (page 66).
- Braised fennel topped with crumbled gorgonzola.
- Caramelized onions and pancetta.
- Wild Mushroom Ragout (page 51).

Wild Mushroom Ragout

In England I used to serve this rich ragout in diamond-shaped puff pastry cases with pastry lids perched on the edge. The mushrooms were the real stars, though, and they make the perfect hot topping for crostini.   MAKES ABOUT 2 CUPS

BRUSH AND/OR WIPE the mushrooms clean. Remove the stems if tough and save for another dish or discard. Slice the mushrooms about ¼ inch thick. In a heavy sauté pan, heat the butter over medium heat, add the mushrooms, and stir for 5 to 6 minutes, or until softened. Add the Madeira, increase the heat to high, and stir until all the liquid has evaporated. Add the cream and stir until the mixture has absorbed the cream and is thick enough to mound. Remove from the heat and stir in the chives.

4 ounces each of 3 kinds of domestic
    and wild mushrooms, such as
    cremini, portobello, shiitake,
    chanterelle, and white button
2 tablespoons unsalted butter
2 tablespoons Madeira wine
2 tablespoons heavy cream
5 chives, cut into ¼-inch lengths
    (about 1 tablespoon)

Deep-fried Polenta Sandwiches

with Spinach and Gorgonzola

These cheesy miracles are a variation on a classic Italian dish. I think of them as alpine mountaineers' finger sandwiches. You could also do this with slivers of fontina instead of the spinach-gorgonzola filling, but I find the spinach adds a green and bracing touch that I would not want to do without. These are very hot when first cooked, probably not a good candidate for finger-food at a stand-up cocktail party. The sandwiches should be accompanied by a robust red wine, preferably Italian, that can hold its own against the strong flavor of the gorgonzola. ✻ *If you want to deep-fry the parsley sprigs for the garnish, they only take a few minutes and are delicate and crunchy. Just make sure the sprigs are completely dry before tossing them into the hot oil.*

MAKES 15 SANDWICHES

SPINACH-GORGONZOLA
FILLING

About 1¼ pounds fresh spinach,
    washed well and stems removed
4 ounces gorgonzola, crumbled
Pinch of nutmeg
Salt and freshly ground black pepper

POLENTA LAYERS

2 cups water
2 cups chicken stock, preferably
    homemade (pages 20–21)
1 teaspoon coarse sea salt
1 cup polenta or coarsely ground
    yellow cornmeal
2 tablespoons unsalted butter
⅓ cup freshly grated Parmesan
Six ½-inch-thick slices mozzarella,
    torn into quarters

TO MAKE THE FILLING: In a large sauté pan, cook the spinach leaves, covered, over low heat with the water that is still clinging to the leaves, until it is wilted and very tender, about 8 minutes. Remove the lid occasionally to toss the leaves so that they cook evenly. Drain the spinach and, when it is cool enough to handle, squeeze it dry and coarsely chop it. Transfer to a bowl, add the gorgonzola, nutmeg, and salt and pepper to taste, and toss together. Set aside.

TO MAKE THE POLENTA: In a large heavy saucepan, bring the water, stock, and salt to a simmer. Sprinkle in the polenta in a very slow, thin stream, whisking constantly in the same direction until all the grains have been incorporated and no lumps remain. Reduce the heat to very low. Switch to a wooden paddle and stir every 1 or 2 minutes for 15 to 20 minutes, or until the mixture comes away from the sides of the pan and the grains of polenta have begun to soften. Stir in the butter and Parmesan until they are evenly distributed. Remove from the heat.

RINSE A 6 x 9-INCH ROASTING PAN with cold water and shake it dry. Working quickly, mound half the polenta in the pan and, using a spatula repeatedly dipped in very hot water, spread into an even layer just over ¼ inch thick. Spread the spinach filling in an even layer over the polenta and distribute the pieces of mozzarella evenly over the filling. Immediately spread the remaining polenta over the filling in an even layer. Cover with a tea towel and let rest for at least 1 hour at room temperature and up to 24 hours in the refrigerator. With a sharp knife, cut the polenta into fifteen 1 x 3-inch strips. Set aside while you make the sauce.

TO MAKE THE SAUCE: In a medium saucepan, heat the olive oil over low heat and sauté the shallots and garlic for 4 to 5 minutes, or until translucent. Add the tomatoes, wine, and water, increase the heat to medium, and simmer, partially covered, until the tomatoes have begun to break down and the mixture is soupy, about 20 minutes. Stir in the butter. (If you do not plan to serve right away, cover and set aside before adding the butter. Just before serving, reheat the sauce if necessary, remove it from the heat, and stir in the butter).

WHEN READY TO SERVE, in a large heavy saucepan or deep-fat fryer, heat about 4 inches of oil to 375°F. Take 3 shallow soup bowls and put the flour in one, the egg and water mixture in the second, and the bread crumbs in the third. Ease the sandwiches out of the roasting pan one by one, gently dredge them in the flour, shaking off the excess, dip both sides into the egg mixture, and coat with the bread crumbs. Using a skimmer, deep-fry the sandwiches in the hot oil for 4 to 5 minutes, or until deep golden. Transfer to a paper towel–lined plate. You will need to do this in 3 batches, keeping the sandwiches warm in a low oven. Return the oil to 375°F before cooking the second and third batches.

MAKE A SMALL POOL of the sauce on each of 5 or 7 heated appetizer plates and overlap 2 or 3 sandwiches on each. Garnish with a sprig of parsley and serve immediately.

NOTE: If canned diced tomatoes are not available, substitute 1 can (14½ ounces) plum tomatoes and break the tomatoes apart with your fingers.

TOMATO SAUCE

2 tablespoons extra virgin olive oil

2 medium shallots, finely chopped

1 clove garlic, minced

1 can (14½ ounces) diced plum tomatoes, drained (see Note)

2 tablespoons dry white wine

2 tablespoons water

2 tablespoons cold unsalted butter, cut into 4 pieces

Vegetable oil, for deep-frying

1 cup all-purpose flour

1 large egg, lightly beaten with ½ cup cold water

1 cup dry bread crumbs

Small sprigs of fresh parsley

Polenta with Shiitake Mushrooms,

Mascarpone, and Salmon Roe

*Christopher Pelham—screenwriter, family friend, and a very talented cook—
created this unusual dish for my book. He wanted a salty, surprising bite in the midst of the soft, warm polenta,
balanced by the coolness of the mascarpone. This is a very sophisticated dish that will really open your eyes—the
existence of the mascarpone and salmon roe are completely unsuspected. Don't delay in serving it, though, otherwise
the contrast of temperatures will be lost.* ✖ *Salmon roe is widely available; the eggs are bright orange and big, about
¼ inch in diameter, and the cost is extremely reasonable when compared with real caviar.*   SERVES 6

2 tablespoons extra virgin olive oil

½ pound shiitake mushrooms, stems
   removed, caps cut into ¼-inch-
   thick slices

3 medium shallots, finely chopped

Salt and freshly ground black pepper

6 cups chicken stock, preferably
   homemade (pages 20-21)

1 teaspoon coarse sea salt

1½ cups polenta or coarsely ground
   yellow cornmeal

½ cup mascarpone (see Note)

4 ounces salmon roe

IN A MEDIUM SKILLET, heat the olive oil over medium heat. Add the
mushrooms and sauté for 2 minutes, or until just slightly wilted. Add the
shallots and sauté for 3 more minutes, stirring occasionally. Stir in salt and
pepper to taste and remove from the heat. Set aside.

IN A LARGE HEAVY SAUCEPAN, bring the stock to a boil and add the
salt. Reduce the heat and, when the liquid is simmering, sprinkle the
polenta evenly over in a very slow, thin stream, whisking constantly in the
same direction until all the grains have been incorporated and no lumps
remain. Reduce the heat to very low. Switch to a wooden paddle and stir
every 1 or 2 minutes for about 30 minutes, or until the mixture pulls away
from the sides of the pan and the grains of polenta have softened. During
the last 2 minutes that the polenta is cooking, return the skillet of
mushrooms to medium-low heat just to heat them through.

SPOON A DOLLOP OF MASCARPONE into the center of each of 6 appetizer
plates and top with a spoonful of salmon roe. Ladle the hot polenta over
the salmon roe and mascarpone, covering it completely. Top each serving
with sautéed mushrooms and serve immediately.

NOTE: Mascarpone is available in Italian groceries and specialty
gourmet markets. Crème fraîche could be substituted.

Lentils and Greens in Broth

with Polenta Croutons

This is one of the dishes that best sum up my attitude about cooking. I wanted to include greens, grains, legumes, dairy, and a small quantity of animal protein, but I wanted beauty, flavor, a balance of textures, and excitement, too. The broth had to be packed with flavor, but I didn't have time to make double chicken stock from scratch, so I used my Quick Chicken Stock with some leftover ham thrown in. Because the lentils are cooked in the broth, it ends up a sort of dark brown, which doesn't bother me because the golden croutons and the bright red tomatoes make up for it with their splashes of color. If you would prefer clear broth, cook the lentils separately in water, drain, and add them to the broth with the kale.

SERVES 6

TO MAKE THE POLENTA CROUTONS: In a large heavy saucepan, heat the olive oil over medium heat. Add the garlic and sage and sauté, stirring occasionally, for about 2 minutes, or until the garlic is softened. Do not let the garlic burn. Add the chicken stock, water, and salt to the pan and bring to a simmer over medium-high heat. When the liquid is simmering, gradually sprinkle the polenta over in a very slow, thin stream, whisking constantly in the same direction until all the grains have been incorporated and no lumps remain. Reduce the heat to low. Switch to a wooden paddle and stir every 1 or 2 minutes for 15 to 20 minutes, or until the mixture pulls away from the side of the pan and the grains of polenta have begun to soften. Stir in the pepper, Parmesan, and butter and mix evenly.

RINSE A 6 x 9-INCH ROASTING PAN with cold water and shake it dry. Mound the polenta in the pan and, using a rubber spatula repeatedly dipped in very hot water, spread the polenta evenly in the pan until it is just under ½ inch thick. Cover with a tea towel and allow to rest for 1 hour at room temperature or up to 24 hours in the refrigerator. Cut the polenta into 1-inch squares. Set aside.

POLENTA CROUTONS

1 tablespoon extra virgin olive oil

2 cloves garlic, minced

5 fresh sage leaves, finely chopped

1 cup chicken stock, preferably homemade (pages 20-21)

1 cup water

1 teaspoon coarse sea salt

½ cup polenta or coarsely ground yellow cornmeal

¼ teaspoon white pepper

¼ cup freshly grated Parmesan

2 tablespoons unsalted butter

2 quarts Quick Chicken Stock (page 21)

½ cup small green lentils, rinsed

1 pound kale, leaves only (see Note)

(cont.)

1½ tablespoons unsalted butter

1 tablespoon canola or vegetable oil

3 plum tomatoes, peeled, seeded, and
cut into ¼-inch dice

HEAT THE STOCK to a slow simmer over medium heat, add the lentils, and simmer for 20 minutes. Bring a large saucepan of lightly salted water to a boil. Blanch the kale leaves for 6 minutes. Plunge the leaves into cold water to stop the cooking process, squeeze them dry, and chop coarsely. Set aside.

HEAT THE BUTTER AND OIL over medium heat in a heavy skillet and, in 2 batches, fry the croutons, nudging occasionally with a spatula to keep them separate and turning once, until crisp and golden at the edges, 8 to 10 minutes. Remove and drain the first batch of croutons on a paper towel–lined plate and keep warm in a low oven while you fry the second.

ADD THE BLANCHED KALE to the broth and simmer for 5 minutes more, or until the lentils are tender but still firm. Ladle into shallow soup bowls and garnish with 4 or 5 of the warm croutons. Garnish each bowl with a little pile of the chopped tomatoes and serve immediately.

NOTE: You may substitute half of a 1-pound package of frozen kale if desired, in which case it is not necessary to blanch. Thaw thoroughly and squeeze dry before adding to the broth.

Cabbage-wrapped Torta

with Leeks and Pancetta

This torta makes a spectacular centerpiece for a late summer buffet, and it looks much more difficult than it really is. The key is not to disturb the cabbage wrapper as you add the hot polenta. Slice and serve the wedges carefully—they can get a little sloppy, but the flavor is the important thing.

SERVES 10

2 large heads savoy cabbage

½ teaspoon coarse sea salt

½ ounce dried porcini mushrooms

2 ounces thinly sliced pancetta, finely chopped (see Note)

¼ cup extra virgin olive oil

2 cloves garlic, minced

2 medium leeks, white and light green parts only, well rinsed and finely chopped

2 cups chicken stock, preferably homemade (pages 20–21)

1½ cups milk

1 teaspoon coarse sea salt

1 cup polenta or coarsely ground yellow cornmeal

¼ cup freshly grated Parmesan

2 tablespoons unsalted butter

½ pound gorgonzola cheese, preferably dolce latte, crumbled

2 tablespoons finely chopped mixed fresh herbs, such as rosemary, parsley, oregano, and basil

SEPARATE THE LARGE OUTER LEAVES of the cabbages, being careful not to tear them; you will need 10 to 15 leaves, depending on the size. Reserve the inner parts of the cabbages for another use. Have ready a large bowl of ice water. Bring a very large saucepan full of water to a boil and add the salt. Blanch the cabbage leaves in the boiling water, three or four at a time, until they are tender but still a beautiful bright green, 3 to 4 minutes. Immediately transfer the blanched leaves to the ice water to stop the cooking and to retain the color. Spread them out carefully on tea towels to drain. Repeat with the remaining leaves.

SOAK THE PORCINI FOR 30 MINUTES in 1 cup of very hot water. Squeeze the mushrooms dry, then chop them coarsely. Strain and reserve the soaking water. Set the mushrooms and the water aside.

BRUSH AN 11-INCH SPRINGFORM PAN with olive oil. Reserve 1 nice cabbage leaf to go in the center of the top. Line the base and sides of the pan with the remaining cabbage leaves, cutting them as necessary to make them fit and making sure there are no gaps. Arrange the leaves so that there is enough hanging over the sides to fold up to cover the torta when it is filled. Set the pan aside.

IN A LARGE HEAVY SAUCEPAN, cook the pancetta over medium heat until the fat is rendered and the pieces are crispy. Transfer to a paper towel–lined plate and wipe the pan clean with another paper towel. Still over medium heat, add the olive oil and, when it is warm, add the garlic and leeks. Sauté, stirring occasionally, until the leeks are softened, about 4 minutes. Do not let the garlic burn. Add the chopped porcini mushrooms and the pancetta and stir for 1 minute more. Add the chicken stock, milk, ½ cup of the mushroom-soaking liquid, and salt and bring the liquid to a simmer over medium-high heat. When the liquid is simmering, gradually sprinkle the polenta over in a very slow, thin stream, whisking constantly in the same direction until all the grains have been incorporated and no lumps remain. Reduce the heat to low. Switch to a wooden paddle and stir every 1 or 2 minutes for 25 to 30 minutes, or until the mixture pulls away from the sides of the pan and the grains of polenta have softened. Add the Parmesan and butter and stir to mix evenly. It will be a fairly loose mixture.

PREHEAT THE OVEN to 275°F.

WHILE THE POLENTA IS STILL WARM and loose, drop half of it, by the spoonful, evenly over the base of the springform pan, on top of the cabbage leaves. You will not be able to spread the polenta without disturbing the cabbage wrapper, so make small dollops and get the bottom layer as even as you can. Jiggle the pan to help it find its level. Quickly scatter the gorgonzola over in an even layer, sprinkle with the chopped herbs, then drop on the remaining polenta, by the spoonful, to form the top layer, making it as even as possible. Wrap the overhanging leaves up and over to enclose the torta, and top with the reserved cabbage leaf.

BAKE THE TORTA for 20 minutes, just to melt the cheese, then allow it to rest for 10 minutes. Remove the sides of the pan, cut the torta into wedges with a sharp serrated knife and serve immediately.

NOTE: Pancetta is available in Italian groceries and specialty gourmet markets. Prosciutto could be substituted.

Gorgonzola Puffs

These nuggets of flavor could be served on tiny doilies or in little paper muffin cups for passing at a cocktail party. Then they can just be popped straight into your mouth. I have found that the only way one person can fill a piping bag without help is as follows: Fit the tip in the bottom of the bag; roll the top of the bag down a few inches and stand it in an empty measuring cup. Spoon the mixture into the bottom of the bag, filling it evenly, then roll up the top and twist it closed.

MAKES 24 PUFFS

Butter or nonstick vegetable oil spray, for preparing the muffin pans

1 tablespoon unsalted butter

1 large shallot, finely chopped

1 cup milk

1½ cups water

1½ teaspoons coarse sea salt

½ cup polenta or coarsely ground yellow cornmeal

Freshly ground white pepper

2 large eggs, separated, at room temperature

½ cup freshly grated Parmesan

3 ounces gorgonzola, crumbled

PREHEAT THE OVEN to 425°F. Butter two 12-cup mini-muffin pans or thoroughly spray them with nonstick vegetable oil spray; set aside.

IN A LARGE HEAVY SAUCEPAN, heat the butter over medium-low heat. Add the shallot and sauté, stirring occasionally, for 3 to 4 minutes, or until softened. Add the milk, water, and salt to the saucepan and bring the liquid to a boil. Reduce the heat and, when the liquid is simmering, gradually sprinkle the polenta over in a very slow, thin stream, whisking constantly in the same direction until no lumps remain. Reduce the heat to very low. Switch to a wooden paddle and stir every 1 or 2 minutes for 15 to 20 minutes, or until the mixture pulls away from the sides of the pan and the grains of polenta have begun to soften. It will be quite a loose mixture. Remove from the heat and stir in the white pepper, egg yolks, Parmesan, and gorgonzola until thoroughly blended.

IN A MIXING BOWL, beat the egg whites to soft peaks. Stir a quarter of the whites thoroughly into the polenta mixture to lighten it, then gently fold in the remaining whites, taking care not to crush too much air out by overfolding. Spoon the mixture into a large piping bag fitted with a ½-inch plain tip. Pipe generous dollops into the muffin pans, finishing each with a point. The puffs should rise about ¼ inch above the surface of the pan.

BAKE FOR 20 MINUTES, or until puffed and golden brown. Remove from the oven and let cool in the pans for 5 minutes. Run a small knife around the edges to release the puffs. Turn them out onto a warmed platter and serve immediately.

Main Attractions

63   *Duck Breasts with Port Sauce and Wild Mushroom Polenta*

66   *Soft Polenta with Braised Italian Sausage, Oven-roasted Tomatoes, and Swiss Chard*

69   *Lamb and Artichoke Stew with Oregano Polenta Dumplings*

71   *Braised Beef Short Ribs over Soft Polenta with Thyme*

74   *Bricked Game Hens with Savoy Cabbage on Polenta Croûtes*

77   *Skewered Chicken Livers, Bacon, and Mushrooms over Polenta Squares*

79   *Polenta Lasagne with Spinach, Zucchini, Herbs, and Fontina*

82   *Pan-fried Trout with Crunchy Polenta Crust*

85   *Chicken Pot Pie with Cornmeal Crust*

87   *Venison Medallions on Cranberry-Orange Polenta Diamonds*

Duck Breasts with Port Sauce
and Wild Mushroom Polenta

When I discovered boneless duck breasts in England years ago, they became my favorite special occasion dish, and this way of cooking them gets rid of almost all the fat! Wait till you see how much you pour off. A word of warning though: Open all the windows as you sauté the duck—it's a smoky process, but worth it. This woodsy polenta is a perfect partner for the rich gaminess of the duck and the port sauce.

SERVES 6

TO MAKE THE POLENTA: Soak the porcini mushrooms in very hot water for 30 minutes, squeeze them dry and coarsely chop them. Strain and reserve the soaking water. Set aside both mushrooms and soaking water.

IN A LARGE HEAVY SAUCEPAN, heat the olive oil over medium heat. Add the onion, white mushrooms, and garlic and sauté, stirring occasionally, for 5 to 6 minutes, or until softened. Add the porcini mushrooms and sauté for 3 minutes more. Add the chicken stock and salt and increase the heat to high. Bring to a boil, reduce the heat and, when the liquid is simmering, sprinkle the polenta over in a very slow, thin stream, whisking constantly in the same direction until all the grains are incorporated and no lumps remain. Reduce the heat to low. Switch to a wooden paddle and stir every 1 or 2 minutes for 25 to 30 minutes, or until the mixture pulls away from the sides of the pan and the grains of polenta have softened. Add the oregano and pepper to taste, then stir in the Parmesan. Taste for seasoning. Hold the polenta in a large metal bowl covered with aluminum foil and set over a smaller pan of gently simmering water while you prepare the duck breasts.

PREHEAT THE OVEN to 400°F. Place a medium roasting pan inside to heat up.

SOFT POLENTA WITH MUSHROOMS

½ ounce dried porcini mushrooms

2 tablespoons olive oil

1 small onion, finely chopped

½ cup coarsely chopped white button mushrooms

3 cloves garlic, minced

4 cups chicken stock, preferably homemade (pages 20-21)

1 teaspoon coarse sea salt

1 cup polenta or coarsely ground yellow cornmeal

1 teaspoon finely chopped fresh oregano

Freshly ground black pepper

⅓ cup freshly grated Parmesan

(cont.)

DUCK BREASTS AND PORT
SAUCE

3 pounds whole boneless duck
    breasts, skin on, halved (2, 2½,
    or 3 breasts)
2 teaspoons canola or vegetable oil
2 shallots, finely chopped
1½ cups soft red wine, such as Merlot
½ cup port
½ cup rich duck or chicken stock
¼ cup crème de cassis
¼ teaspoon table salt
Pinch of freshly ground black pepper
4 tablespoons (½ stick) cold unsalted
    butter, cut into 8 pieces

TO COOK THE DUCK AND MAKE THE SAUCE: Using a very sharp knife, score the skin of the duck breasts in several places, being careful not to cut into the flesh. In a large heavy sauté pan, heat the oil over medium-high heat. When it is very hot, place the duck breasts, skin side down, into the pan. Cook for 5 to 6 minutes, pouring off the rendered fat halfway through; the skin should be brown and crispy. Place the breasts, flesh side down, in the roasting pan in the hot oven. Cook for 8 to 10 minutes more, depending on how pink you like your duck, and then remove to a cutting board. Loosely cover with foil and allow to rest for 5 minutes.

WHILE THE DUCK IS COOKING in the oven, pour off the remaining fat and discard it. Wipe the pan clean with a paper towel and add the shallots, red wine, port, stock, crème de cassis, salt, and pepper. Over high heat, boil the liquid rapidly to reduce it by about two-thirds, to barely a cup. The sauce should be almost syrupy. Remove the pan from the heat, add the cubed butter all at once and whisk constantly until the butter is absorbed.

SLICE THE DUCK BREASTS across the grain into ¾-inch slices. Mound some of the polenta on each of 6 warmed dinner plates. Arrange the sliced duck breast next to it and drizzle a little of the sauce over each portion of the duck. Serve at once.

Soft Polenta with Braised Italian Sausage,

Oven-roasted Tomatoes, and Swiss Chard

I learned about these oven-roasted tomatoes while working on the Patina restaurant cookbook and they have been part of my repertoire ever since. They give this dish its deep, intense flavor and there is really no substitute. Be sure to make the tomatoes at least six hours ahead. It is worth doubling the quantity to three pounds and keeping the other half for pasta, hors d'oeuvres, or even as a topping for cottage cheese. Keep the leftover tomatoes wrapped in plastic in the refrigerator. For best results the tomatoes should be eaten within five days, though they can be frozen. SERVES 6

OVEN-ROASTED TOMATOES

1½ pounds plum tomatoes, stem
  ends removed, halved, and seeds
  scraped out

Coarse sea salt and freshly ground
  black pepper

2 tablespoons extra virgin olive oil

CHARD AND SAUSAGE SAUCE

1 pound Swiss chard

¾ pound sweet Italian sausage,
  cut into 1-inch lengths

¾ pound hot Italian sausage,
  cut into 1-inch lengths

2 tablespoons extra virgin olive oil

1 medium onion, finely chopped

1 small carrot, finely chopped

5 leaves fresh sage, minced

2 cloves garlic, minced

1 cup dry white wine

2 tablespoons tomato paste

PREHEAT THE OVEN to 200°F.

TO MAKE THE OVEN-ROASTED TOMATOES: Brush a large baking sheet with olive oil and lay the tomatoes on it in a single layer, cut side up. Sprinkle them with salt and pepper, then turn cut side down. Brush the tops of the tomatoes with olive oil and sprinkle with salt and pepper. Roast for 4 to 6 hours, regulating the heat so that it doesn't get so hot that the tomatoes burn. Since the tomatoes must cook at a very low and constant temperature, it is best to use an oven thermometer. Prop the oven open by 1 inch with a dish towel if the temperature is difficult to regulate at such a low heat. The tomatoes are done when they are shrunken, dehydrated, and shriveled on top but still quite juicy underneath. Cool on the baking sheet and wrap with plastic wrap until needed.

TO MAKE THE SAUCE: Rinse and drain the Swiss chard. Remove the leaves from the ribs, trim and discard the woody bottoms, and slice the ribs ⅜ inch thick. Coarsely chop the leaves and set both aside separately.

IN A LARGE HEAVY SAUTÉ PAN, cook all the sausages over medium-low heat for about 15 minutes, stirring occasionally, or until no trace of pink remains. With a slotted spoon, remove the sausage to a bowl, then pour off and discard the fat from the pan. Wipe the pan with a paper towel. Over medium heat, combine the olive oil, onion, and carrot and sauté for 6 to 8 minutes, or until the onion is translucent. Return the sausage to the

(cont.)

POLENTA WITH WILD MUSHROOMS

½ ounce dried porcini mushrooms

2 tablespoons extra virgin olive oil

1 small onion, finely chopped

2 cloves garlic, minced

3 cups chicken stock, preferably
  homemade (pages 20-21)

1 teaspoon coarse sea salt

1 cup polenta or coarsely ground
  yellow cornmeal

3 tablespoons unsalted butter

Freshly ground black pepper

¾ cup freshly grated Parmesan

pan, add the sage and garlic, and stir for 2 minutes. Add half the wine and half the tomato paste and stir until most of the wine has evaporated. Cut the oven-roasted tomatoes in half lengthwise and then again cross-wise. Add them to the pan. Add the remaining wine, remaining tomato paste, and the ribs of the Swiss chard. Cover the pan and cook, stirring occasionally, for 10 minutes. Remove from the heat, cover, and set aside while you cook the polenta.

SOAK THE PORCINI MUSHROOMS in 1 cup of very hot water for 30 minutes, squeeze dry and finely chop them. Strain the soaking water. Set aside both mushrooms and soaking water.

TO MAKE THE POLENTA: In a large heavy saucepan, heat the olive oil over medium heat. Add the onion and garlic and sauté, stirring occasionally, for 5 to 6 minutes, or until softened. Add the porcini to the pan and stir for 1 minute more. Add the chicken stock, the mushroom-soaking liquid, and salt and increase the heat to high. When the liquid is simmering, gradually sprinkle the polenta over in a very slow, thin stream, whisking constantly in the same direction until all the grains are incorporated and no lumps remain. Reduce the heat to very low. Switch to a wooden paddle and stir every 1 or 2 minutes for 25 to 30 minutes, or until the mixture pulls away from the sides of the pan and the grains of polenta have softened. Stir in the butter, pepper to taste, and Parmesan and remove from the heat.

RETURN THE SAUCE TO MEDIUM-HIGH HEAT, add the Swiss chard leaves and cover. After 2 minutes, remove the lid and stir to mix. Repeat twice more and, after about 6 minutes when the chard leaves are tender, remove from the heat. Mound some of the soft polenta onto each of 6 heated dinner plates, make a well in the center and spoon the sauce over.

Lamb and Artichoke Stew

with Oregano Polenta Dumplings

Lamb and artichokes are two made-for-each-other ingredients whose appearance marks the beginning of spring in Greece and throughout the Mediterranean. This hearty stew with its herb dumplings would be perfect for a rainy Sunday in March. The juices are slightly thickened because the lamb pieces are floured before browning. If you prefer a thin stew, leave out the flour and brown the lamb with just a light seasoning of salt and pepper. Serve with plenty of crusty bread to soak up the rich sauce. The stew can be made a day in advance; in fact, as with all braises, the flavor will improve. Reheat the stew while making the dumpling mixture and proceed.

SERVES 6

PREHEAT THE OVEN to 325°F.

TO MAKE THE STEW: In a large heavy skillet, heat the oil over medium heat and sauté the onion for 5 to 6 minutes, or until softened and just slightly browned. With a slotted spoon, transfer it to a large cast iron and enamel casserole with a lid.

PLACE THE FLOUR in a large shallow bowl and season with ½ teaspoon salt and ½ teaspoon pepper. Dry the lamb pieces thoroughly with paper towels, toss them in the flour and shake briefly in a colander to remove the excess. In the same pan, sauté the lamb over medium-high heat until brown, in 2 or 3 batches to prevent overcrowding. Add more oil if necessary. Turn the lamb with tongs to be sure all sides are browned evenly and to prevent scorching. As each batch of lamb is done, transfer it to the casserole. When finished, deglaze the skillet with the wine and pour the wine over the lamb. Add the garlic, oregano, and enough stock to barely cover the ingredients. Cover the casserole. Bring the liquid to a simmer on the top of the stove. Transfer the casserole to the oven and bake for 20 minutes.

QUARTER THE ARTICHOKES, cut off the top half, and trim away the leaves and chokes. Soak the artichokes in cold water acidulated with

LAMB STEW

2 tablespoons canola or vegetable oil

1 large yellow onion, thinly sliced

½ cup all-purpose flour

Salt and freshly ground black pepper

2½ pounds boneless lamb, from the shoulder, cut into 1 x 2-inch pieces

1½ cups Riesling wine

2 large cloves garlic, minced

1 sprig of fresh oregano

2½ cups chicken or beef stock, or as needed

7 medium artichokes, (about 12 ounces each) or 1 package (nine ounces) frozen artichoke hearts, thawed

Juice of 1 lemon

18 baby carrots, trimmed

(cont.)

OREGANO POLENTA
DUMPLINGS

1 cup flour

½ cup polenta or coarsely ground
    yellow cornmeal

2 teaspoons baking powder

½ teaspoon salt

2 teaspoons finely chopped fresh
    oregano or 1 scant teaspoon
    dried oregano, crumbled

1 tablespoon freshly grated Parmesan

2 tablespoons cold unsalted butter,
    cut into small cubes

¾ cup milk

lemon juice. Add the carrots to the casserole and cook for 25 minutes more (if you plan to serve the stew the same day, make the dumpling mixture while the stew is cooking). Add the artichokes and return the casserole to the oven, uncovered, for 10 minutes more. Transfer it to the top of the stove. If you plan to serve the stew the following day, cool to room temperature as quickly as possible and refrigerate. If not, skim the fat with a spoon, then drag a paper towel across the top to remove the last bit of fat. Set aside while you make the dumpling mixture. (If the stew has been refrigerated, skim it, then warm it over medium-low heat while you make the dumpling mixture.)

TO MAKE THE DUMPLINGS: In a medium bowl, stir together the flour, polenta, baking powder, salt, oregano, and Parmesan until blended. Work the butter into the mixture with your fingertips until it is the consistency of coarse bread crumbs. With a fork, stir in the milk until it is a thick and clumpy batter.

RETURN THE STEW TO A SIMMER over medium heat and drop the dumpling mixture in 12 fairly equal spoonfuls over the top of the simmering stew. Do not stir. Cover, reduce the heat to medium-low, and simmer for about 10 minutes, or until the dumplings are firm. The lamb should be firm but not tough. Ladle the stew into 6 warmed shallow soup bowls, making sure each person gets 2 dumplings.

Braised Beef Short Ribs

over Soft Polenta with Thyme

It is always the toughest, fattiest cuts of beef that have the most flavor. Sad but true. This long slow braise tenderizes the ribs, but it is the high-heat searing at the very beginning that allows you to get rid of most of the fat. The aromas that waft through the kitchen after you add the aromatic vegetables to the pan are likely to bring the neighbors running—luckily this recipe can be doubled or even tripled. In fact, the flavor will improve if the dish is left to stand for up to a day. Gently reheat it in the oven while you cook the polenta. This thyme-infused creamy polenta makes the perfect foil for the rich juices of the beef and the tender meat. SERVES 6

PREHEAT THE OVEN to 450°F.

TO COOK THE RIBS: Mix the flour, cumin, salt, and pepper to taste together in a bowl. Dredge the beef ribs thoroughly, then toss in a colander to shake off the excess. In a roasting pan, sear the pieces, bone side up, in the oven for 30 minutes, then pour off and discard the fat.

ADD THE CARROT, onion, thyme, and bay leaves and return the pan to the oven for 10 minutes more. Add the broth and wine, reduce the oven to 350°F, and cover the pan with a lid or with foil. Braise the beef for 1 hour, turning the pieces over halfway through the cooking time. Remove the lid and cook for 15 minutes more, basting twice. If you plan to serve the ribs the next day, cool to room temperature as quickly as possible and refrigerate. If not, skim the fat with a spoon, then with a paper towel dragged across the surface. (Skim refrigerated stew before reheating.)

ABOUT 45 MINUTES BEFORE SERVING, make the polenta. This can be done while the meat is cooking in the oven or while it is being reheated in a 325°F oven. In a large heavy saucepan, heat the olive oil over medium heat. Add the onion and garlic and sauté, stirring occasionally, for 5 to 6 minutes, or until softened. Add the chicken stock, water, and salt to the pan and increase the heat to medium-high. When the liquid is simmering, gradually sprinkle the polenta over in a very slow, thin stream, whisking

BRAISED BEEF RIBS

2 tablespoons all-purpose flour

1 teaspoon ground cumin

Coarse sea salt and freshly ground
  black pepper

4 pounds beef short ribs, cut into
  3-inch lengths

1 large carrot, quartered lengthwise
  and cut into 2-inch lengths

1 medium onion, quartered

1 large sprig of thyme or ¼ teaspoon
  dried thyme, crumbled

2 bay leaves

2 cups beef broth

1 cup dry white wine

(cont.)

SOFT POLENTA WITH THYME

2 tablespoons extra virgin olive oil

1 medium onion, finely chopped

3 cloves garlic, minced

4½ cups chicken stock, preferably
    homemade (pages 20-21)

1½ cups water

1½ teaspoons coarse sea salt

1½ cups polenta or coarsely ground
    yellow cornmeal

4 tablespoons (½ stick) unsalted
    butter

2 teaspoons finely chopped fresh
    thyme leaves or scant 1 teaspoon
    dried thyme, crumbled

Freshly ground black pepper

½ cup freshly grated Parmesan

constantly in the same direction until all the grains are incorporated and no lumps remain. Reduce the heat to very low. Switch to a wooden paddle and stir thoroughly every 1 or 2 minutes for 25 to 30 minutes, or until the mixture pulls away from the sides of the pan and the grains of polenta have softened. Stir in the butter, thyme, pepper to taste, and Parmesan and remove from the heat.

SPOON SOME POLENTA into each of 6 warmed shallow soup bowls and top with a few ribs, vegetables, and a generous spoonful of the sauce.

Bricked Game Hens

with Savoy Cabbage on Polenta Croûtes

"Bricked" quail, rabbit, and chicken, long popular dishes in northern Italy, have now been adopted by some American restaurants. When I first saw it on a menu, though, it was a little daunting, even for me. The idea is to sauté a spatchcocked bird (or rabbit) with a brick on top to press it down onto the heat. (Spatchcocked means the backbone is removed and the bird is flattened.) The result is that the awkwardly shaped bird cooks faster, cooks more evenly, and comes out in a nice flat shape. Any flavors added are compressed right into the flesh as it cooks. ⚜ It is, of course, not necessary to use a brick for this operation. A heavy pan of a slightly smaller diameter than the cooking pan works just as well. This is a fairly complicated dish, but by following the instructions carefully during the final presentation you should have no problem. This is one of those times, though, when you will not want to have helpful guests crowding the kitchen, drinks in hand, peering inquisitively into every pan. ⚜ As this is a complex dish, the only thing that is needed as an accompaniment is a salad of slivered fennel or belgian endive with whole parsley leaves and a simple lemon vinaigrette, which can be ready and waiting in the refrigerator.

SERVES 4

FLAVORING PASTE AND
MARINADE

2 cornish game hens (about 1 pound
    each)

1 ounce pancetta, finely chopped
    (see Note)

2 cloves garlic, thinly sliced

1 tablespoon finely chopped fresh
    rosemary

Freshly ground black pepper

2 tablespoons extra virgin olive oil

½ cup dry provençal-style rosé wine,
    such as dry grenache, rosé of
    cabernet, or Bonny Doon's Vin
    Gris, but not white zinfandel

TO PREPARE THE HENS: Rinse the hens with cold water, pat dry, and remove any excess fat from around the vent. Remove the backbones with sharp kitchen shears and remove the wishbone from between the top of the breasts with a small, sharp knife. With the hens breast up, push down to flatten them with the palm of your hand, breaking some of the rib bones.

MAKE A PASTE with the pancetta, garlic, rosemary, pepper to taste, and olive oil. Smear the paste all over the hens, loosening the skin of the breast and thigh to push some of the paste underneath. Place the hens in a large zip-lock bag and pour in the wine. Seal the bag and slosh the wine around so that it comes into contact with all surfaces of the birds. Refrigerate for 2 hours.

TO MAKE THE POLENTA: In a medium-size heavy saucepan, combine the milk, water, stock, and salt and bring the mixture to a boil. Reduce the heat and, when the liquid is simmering, sprinkle in the polenta in a very slow, thin stream, whisking constantly in the same direction until all the grains have been incorporated and no lumps remain. Reduce the heat to very low. Switch to a wooden paddle and stir once every 1 or 2 minutes for 15 to 20 minutes, or until the mixture comes away from the sides of the pan and the grains of polenta have begun to soften. The mixture should be so thick that the paddle will stand straight upright for 2 or 3 seconds. Stir in the pepper, butter, and Parmesan until they are evenly distributed and remove from the heat.

RINSE A 6 x 9-INCH ROASTING PAN with cold water and shake it dry. Mound the polenta in the pan and, using a spatula repeatedly dipped in very hot water, spread the polenta into an even layer about ¾ inch thick. Cover with a tea towel and let rest for at least 1 hour at room temperature or for up to 24 hours in the refrigerator.

TO COOK THE HENS: Remove the hens from the refrigerator and let them come to room temperature, about 30 minutes. Pat dry with paper towels and discard the marinade and the bag. In a 12-inch skillet, heat 3 tablespoons of the olive oil over medium-high heat. Have ready a 10-inch skillet with a clean base and a few cans or stones in it for weights. When the oil is hot, add the hens to the pan, skin side down, and immediately put the 10-inch skillet on top to weight them down. Cook for about 10 minutes, regulating the heat so that the hens are actively sautéing but not burning. Turn the hens over and weight again, reducing the heat to medium about 1 minute after turning. Cook for another 8 to 10 minutes, or until the juices from the thigh joint run clear. Remove from the heat, cover with aluminum foil, and keep warm in a low oven while you prepare the polenta croûtes and the cabbage.

PREHEAT AN INDOOR BROILER or an outdoor grill to high heat.

POLENTA CROÛTES

1 cup milk

1 cup water

1 cup chicken stock, preferably homemade (pages 20-21)

1 scant teaspoon coarse sea salt

1 cup polenta or coarsely ground yellow cornmeal

¼ teaspoon white pepper

2 tablespoons unsalted butter

¼ cup freshly grated Parmesan

5 tablespoons extra virgin olive oil

2 tablespoons unsalted butter, melted

Freshly ground black pepper

½ large head savoy cabbage, tough outer leaves removed, thinly sliced

1 medium shallot, finely chopped

¼ cup chicken stock

¼ teaspoon table salt

2 tablespoons whole-grain mustard

(cont.)

CUT THE POLENTA into four 3-inch rounds with a cookie cutter or a large glass, brush evenly with the melted butter, and sprinkle with black pepper to taste. Grill about 3 inches from the hot grill or broiler for 6 to 7 minutes on each side, or until browned and crisp.

WHILE YOU ARE GRILLING THE POLENTA, in a large heavy skillet with a tight-fitting lid, heat the remaining 2 tablespoons of olive oil over medium-high heat. Add the cabbage, shallot, ¼ cup chicken stock, and salt. Cover and cook for 4 minutes. Toss, so that the cooked cabbage is on top, cover, reduce the heat to medium-low, and cook for 3 to 5 minutes more, or until all the cabbage is tender but still bright green. Stir in the mustard and remove from the heat.

PLACE A POLENTA CROÛTE in the center of each of 4 heated dinner plates. Halve the game hens lengthwise through the breastbone and perch a halved hen over 1 side of the croûte, arrange some of the cabbage around the other side, and serve immediately.

NOTES: Quail may be substituted for the game hens if they are readily available. Allow two per person and reduce the cooking time to 4 or 5 minutes, turning once.

Pancetta is available in Italian groceries and specialty gourmet markets. Prosciutto could be substituted.

Skewered Chicken Livers, Bacon, and Mushrooms

over Polenta Squares

This is a rich dish that would definitely have appealed to my English in-laws and friends. If you are not a fan of chicken liver, it is equally delicious made with boneless chicken breasts. Or, if you're on the fence about it, use half chicken livers and half chicken breasts. A salad is all that is needed to round out this hearty outdoor repast, but be sure to use strong greens such as endive and radicchio to stand up to the strong flavor of the chicken liver. A hefty Rhône-style wine, such as Bonny Doon's Cigar Volant, would be perfect.

SERVES 6

TO MAKE THE POLENTA SQUARES: In a large heavy saucepan, heat the olive oil over low heat. Add the garlic and sauté, stirring constantly, for about 3 minutes, or until it is softened. Do not let the garlic burn. Add the chicken stock, water, and salt and bring to a simmer over medium-high heat. When the liquid is simmering, gradually sprinkle the polenta over in a very slow, thin stream, whisking constantly in the same direction until all the grains have been incorporated and no lumps remain. Reduce the heat to very low. Switch to a wooden paddle and stir thoroughly every 1 or 2 minutes for 25 to 30 minutes, or until the mixture pulls away from the sides of the pan and the grains of polenta have softened. Stir in the pepper, Parmesan, parsley, and butter. The mixture will be very thick.

RINSE AN 8 x 12-INCH ROASTING PAN with cold water, shake it dry and mound the polenta in it. Using a rubber spatula repeatedly dipped in very hot water, spread the polenta evenly in the pan until it is just under ½ inch thick. Cover with a tea towel and allow to rest for 1 hour at room temperature, or up to 24 hours in the refrigerator.

TO PREPARE THE CHICKEN LIVERS: In a large bowl, combine the olive oil, garlic, thyme, salt, and pepper and mix. Add the bacon, mushrooms, and chicken livers and toss to coat evenly. Let stand, covered with a tea towel, for 5 to 10 minutes, or refrigerate for up to 30 minutes. Thread the

6 bamboo skewers soaked for 2 hours
  in water to cover

POLENTA SQUARES

2 teaspoons extra virgin olive oil

2 cloves garlic, minced

2 cups chicken stock, preferably
  homemade (pages 20-21)

1 cup water

1 teaspoon coarse sea salt

1 cup polenta or coarsely ground
  yellow cornmeal

Freshly ground black pepper

3 tablespoons freshly grated
  Parmesan

2 tablespoons finely chopped parsley

1½ tablespoons unsalted butter

(cont.)

CHICKEN LIVERS

2 tablespoons extra virgin olive oil

1 clove garlic, put through a
    garlic press

2 teaspoons finely chopped
    fresh thyme

½ teaspoon table salt

½ teaspoon freshly ground
    black pepper

6 slices bacon, cut into 1-inch pieces

18 large firm white button
    mushrooms

1½ pounds chicken livers, cut into
    approximately 1-inch cubes

1 tablespoon extra virgin olive oil, for
    brushing the polenta squares

Lemon wedges, for garnish

ingredients alternately onto the skewers, cutting the mushrooms in half if they are too large and making sure each skewer contains an equal amount of each ingredient. Leave enough space at the base of each skewer to give you room to grab it, and keep the ingredients snugly together so that the bacon bastes the other ingredients as they cook. (The skewers may be refrigerated, covered, for up to 1 hour.)

WHEN READY TO SERVE, preheat an outdoor grill or indoor broiler to high heat.

CUT THE POLENTA into six 4-inch squares. Brush the squares with olive oil and grill or broil for about 7 minutes on each side, or until golden. Keep warm in a low oven on a paper towel–lined plate while you grill the skewers for 2 to 3 minutes on each of all 4 sides, or until the bacon is crispy and the livers are browned outside but still slightly pink inside. Place a polenta square on each of 6 warmed dinner plates and top with one of the skewers. Garnish the plate with lemon wedges and serve immediately.

Polenta Lasagne

with Spinach, Zucchini, Herbs, and Fontina

This is a variation of pasticciata, a traditional northern Italian polenta dish that is often made with cheese only. The addition of vegetables and fresh herbs gives it a nice summery flavor. A fairly substantial dish, it requires nothing more than a green salad liberally scattered with halved red and yellow cherry tomatoes, dressed with a simple lemon-juice vinaigrette, to accompany it. A light red wine, such as a Valpolicella, would round out the menu nicely. This dish may take a little time to prepare, but it's healthy eating at its very best.

SERVES 6

TO MAKE THE POLENTA: In a very large heavy saucepan, heat the olive oil over very low heat. Add the garlic and sauté, stirring constantly, for about 3 minutes, or until softened. Do not let the garlic burn. Add the chicken stock, water, and salt and bring to a boil. Reduce the heat and, when the liquid is simmering, gradually sprinkle the polenta over in a very slow, thin stream, whisking constantly in the same direction until all the grains have been incorporated and no lumps remain. Reduce the heat to very low. Switch to a wooden paddle and stir every 1 or 2 minutes for 20 to 25 minutes, or until the mixture pulls away from the sides of the pan and the grains of polenta have softened. Stir in the butter. The mixture will be very thick.

RINSE 2 LARGE BAKING SHEETS with cold water and shake them dry. Mound half the polenta on each one. Using a rubber spatula repeatedly dipped in very hot water, spread the polenta evenly in the pans until it is just over ¼ inch thick. Cover the pans with tea towels and allow to rest for 1 hour at room temperature or up to 24 hours in the refrigerator.

TO MAKE THE FILLING: In a large skillet, heat the olive oil over medium heat and sauté the onion for 4 to 5 minutes, stirring, or until it is softened. Add the zucchini and mushrooms and stir for 3 to 4 minutes more, or until the vegetables begin to soften. Season with salt and pepper

POLENTA LAYERS

1 tablespoon extra virgin olive oil

2 cloves garlic, finely chopped

3 cups chicken stock, preferably homemade (pages 20-21)

3 cups water

1 teaspoon coarse sea salt

1½ cups polenta or coarsely ground yellow cornmeal

3 tablespoons unsalted butter

VEGETABLE FILLING

2 tablespoons extra virgin olive oil

1 medium-size white or yellow onion, coarsely chopped

3 medium zucchini, cut into ¼-inch dice

6 ounces white button mushrooms, wiped clean and sliced ¼ inch thick

(cont.)

to taste. Add half the spinach, cover the pan, reduce the heat to low, and cook for 2 minutes. Turn the spinach over so that the wilted leaves are on top and add the remaining spinach. Cook, covered, for 2 minutes more, and turn the spinach. Repeat until all the spinach has wilted. Add the fresh herbs, cover, and cook for 1 minute more. Remove from the heat.

PREHEAT THE OVEN to 375°F. Butter the bottom and sides of a large, deep baking dish, attractive enough to serve at the table, either a 10 x 14 x 2-inch rectangular dish or a 13 x 9-inch oval dish.

CUT THE POLENTA into 2 x 4-inch rectangles. Layer the ingredients in the following order: polenta rectangles, ricotta sprinkled with Parmesan, another layer of polenta, vegetable filling, ricotta sprinkled with fontina, and another layer of polenta. Continue layering until you have used up all the ingredients, finishing with a thin layer of the vegetable filling sprinkled with Parmesan and black pepper to taste. Tap the baking dish gently on the counter to settle the ingredients.

BAKE FOR 35 MINUTES, or until the top is golden brown. Let stand for about 7 minutes. Cut into loosely defined wedges and serve immediately.

Salt and freshly ground black pepper
1 pound fresh spinach leaves, well washed, shaken dry, and coarsely chopped
2 tablespoons finely chopped fresh marjoram
2 tablespoons finely chopped fresh basil

Butter, for preparing the baking dish
2 cups (15-ounce container) fresh ricotta, at room temperature
½ cup freshly grated Parmesan or romano
½ pound Italian fontina, slivered
Freshly ground black pepper

Pan-fried Trout

with Crunchy Polenta Crust

This is a simple dish, in the tradition of both rustic Italian cooking and the down-home cooking of the deep South. I like the fish garnished simply, with only parsley and lemon wedges, but you could also serve it on a small pool of the Tomato Sauce on page 53. You will need two large skillets to fry the fish; they can't be crowded in the pan, otherwise the fish will steam instead of fry quickly, and the crust may fall off. Because of this, it isn't really viable to cook more than four fish. Of course, this is only worth doing if your trout are unquestionably fresh!

SERVES 4

4 cleaned whole trout (12 to 16 ounces each)

1½ cups milk

1¼ cups polenta or coarsely ground yellow cornmeal

½ cup all-purpose flour

1 teaspoon finely chopped parsley

Coarse sea salt and freshly ground black pepper

6 tablespoons olive oil

6 tablespoons canola or vegetable oil

Sprigs of fresh parsley and lemon wedges, for garnish

RINSE THE TROUT under cold running water. Place the milk in a shallow baking dish long enough to accommodate the whole fish. In a roasting pan, combine the polenta, flour, parsley, 1 teaspoon salt, and ½ teaspoon pepper and toss to mix evenly.

IN EACH OF 2 HEAVY SKILLETS, preferably cast-iron, heat 3 tablespoons of the olive oil and 3 tablespoons of the canola oil over medium-high heat until it is very hot but not smoking. Quickly dip both sides of each fish in the milk and then dredge them in the polenta mixture, sprinkling the cavities of the fish with additional salt and pepper and patting the outside of the fish lightly to help the mixture adhere. Fry 2 fish in each skillet for about 5 minutes on each side, using a metal spatula to turn the fish. Serve immediately, garnished with fresh parsley and lemon wedges.

Chicken Pot Pie with Cornmeal Crust

Sometimes you just need a chicken pot pie. I learned to love savory pies during my years in England. Cornish pasties, raised game pies with a hot-water crust, steak and kidney pudding with a suet crust—these are rich, substantial meals designed to satisfy a big hunger in a cold climate. This pie is silky and rich, but I've streamlined it by substituting milk for cream in the velouté sauce and sautéing the onions and mushrooms in vegetable oil instead of butter. But it's still plenty satisfying!

SERVES 6

TO MAKE THE CORNMEAL CRUST: In a food processor fitted with the metal blade, combine the flour, cornmeal, baking powder, and salt and process just to mix. Add the butter and process in short bursts, scraping down the sides of the bowl as necessary, until the mixture resembles coarse bread crumbs. Add the whole egg, egg yolk, lemon zest, and 1 tablespoon ice water and process again for a few short bursts, scraping down the sides, until the dough just comes together, but is still a bit crumbly. If the dough seems very dry, sprinkle up to 1 more tablespoon of water over the mixture. Do not overprocess or the crust will be tough. Turn the dough out onto a lightly floured surface and work together into a ball the consistency of stiff Play-Doh, press down into a round disk, and wrap with plastic. Refrigerate the dough for at least 1 hour or overnight.

TO MAKE THE FILLING: In a medium saucepan, bring the chicken stock to a simmer, add the carrots and thyme, and simmer for 4 minutes. Strain the stock into a heatproof jug and set aside. Remove and discard the thyme. Set the carrots aside.

IN A MEDIUM SKILLET, heat the vegetable oil over medium heat and sauté the onion and the mushrooms, stirring occasionally, for about 10 minutes, or until they are tender and most of the liquid has evaporated. Add salt and pepper to taste, remove from the heat and set aside.

DRY THE SAUCEPAN you used to cook the carrots. Add the butter and heat it over medium heat. Remove from the heat and stir in the flour to

CORNMEAL CRUST

2 cups all-purpose flour

2/3 cup medium-grind yellow cornmeal (see Note)

1 teaspoon baking powder

1/2 teaspoon table salt

12 tablespoons (1 1/2 sticks) cold un-salted butter, cut into small cubes

1 large egg

1 large egg yolk

1 1/2 teaspoons grated lemon zest

1 tablespoon ice water, or more as needed

CHICKEN FILLING

4 1/2 cups chicken stock, preferably homemade (pages 20-21)

3 medium carrots, sliced 1/4 inch thick

3 sprigs of fresh thyme

2 tablespoons canola or vegetable oil

1/2 yellow onion, finely chopped

(cont.)

85

¾ pound white button mushrooms,
   halved or quartered if very large

Salt and freshly ground black pepper

4 tablespoons (½ stick) unsalted
   butter

¼ cup all-purpose flour

½ cup milk

16 fresh pearl onions, peeled and
   blanched for 5 minutes in boiling
   water, or 16 frozen pearl onions,
   thawed

¼ cup finely chopped parsley

1 pound slightly undercooked poached
   chicken breasts or boneless
   leftover chicken, cut into ¾-inch
   chunks (about 3 cups)

1 tablespoon fresh lemon juice

Butter, for preparing the baking dish

2 tablespoons milk

make a thick paste. Return the pan to the heat and stir the flour roux until it is bubbling but not brown, about 3 to 4 minutes. Gradually add the reserved chicken stock all at once, stirring until the mixture is smooth. Add the milk and simmer the sauce for 15 minutes, or until it is thickened, stirring occasionally to keep the sauce at the bottom of the pan from scorching. Remove from the heat and stir in the carrots, mushrooms, pearl onions, parsley, chicken, and lemon juice. Taste and adjust the seasoning.

PREHEAT THE OVEN to 375°F. Butter the bottom and sides but not the top edge of a round or oval ceramic baking dish, about 1½-quart capacity, and set it aside.

QUICKLY ROLL OUT THE DOUGH between 2 large sheets of plastic wrap to a size that will fit over your baking dish. The crust will have a rough and rustic appearance. Refrigerate the rolled dough for 20 minutes more, or until it is firm again.

TURN THE CHICKEN FILLING into the baking dish and brush the top edge of the dish with some of the milk. Place the rolled dough on a work surface next to the baking dish and peel away the top sheet of plastic wrap. Gently invert the dough over the baking dish, using the plastic to transfer it, then peel away the remaining plastic. Gently press the edges to secure them to the dish. With a sharp knife, cut 2 steam vents in the top, then brush the top of the dough lightly with milk.

BAKE THE PIE for 20 minutes, then reduce the heat to 300°F. Continue to bake for 10 to 15 minutes more, or until the crust is shiny and golden. Allow to stand for 10 minutes before serving.

NOTES: Polenta may be substituted for the medium-grind cornmeal for a really toothsome crust. Add 1 or 2 extra tablespoons of water when making up the dough.

Venison Medallions

on Cranberry-Orange Polenta Diamonds

This is the ultimate wintertime special occasion dish. With its brightly hued cranberries against a golden backdrop of polenta, its rich flavor of venison, and its heady aroma of oranges mixed with pinot noir, this is a dish that will thrill all your senses. Serve with the same wine that went into the sauce. SERVES 6

TO MAKE THE VENISON STOCK: In a large saucepan, combine all the ingredients for the stock and bring to a simmer over medium heat. Skim off any impurities and froth that rise to the surface, partially cover, and simmer for 1½ hours. Strain through a strainer lined with a double thickness of slightly dampened cheesecloth into a clean pan and discard the solids. Bring to a simmer and reduce by half, so that 2 cups of liquid remain. Set aside. (The stock may be refrigerated for up to 2 days or frozen for up to 3 months.)

TO MAKE THE POLENTA: In a large heavy saucepan, combine the oil and the pancetta and cook over low heat for 3 to 4 minutes, or until the pancetta has rendered its fat. Add the onion and garlic, and cook, stirring, for 4 to 5 minutes, or until softened. Add the orange zest and stir for 1 minute more. Add the water, 1 cup of the reserved venison stock, orange juice, and salt to the pan and bring the liquid to a boil. Reduce the heat and, when the liquid is simmering, gradually sprinkle the polenta over in a very slow, thin stream, whisking constantly in the same direction until all the grains have been incorporated and no lumps remain. Reduce the heat to low. Switch to a wooden paddle and stir every 1 or 2 minutes for 25 to 30 minutes, or until the mixture pulls away from the sides of the pan and the grains of polenta have softened. Stir in the butter, dried cranberries, and pepper. The mixture will be very thick.

VENISON STOCK

1 quart beef stock, homemade or
   good quality storebought

3 pounds venison bones

1 medium carrot, coarsely chopped

3 bay leaves

10 juniper berries, crushed

1 sprig of fresh rosemary

POLENTA DIAMONDS

1 tablespoon extra virgin olive oil

1 ounce pancetta, coarsely chopped

½ medium-size red onion,
   finely chopped

1 clove garlic, finely chopped

Grated zest of 1 orange

3 cups water

Juice of 1 orange

1 scant teaspoon coarse sea salt

1 cup polenta or coarsely ground
   yellow cornmeal

(cont.)

4 tablespoons (½ stick) unsalted
    butter, cut into ½-inch cubes
½ cup dried cranberries
Freshly ground black pepper

2 tablespoons unsalted butter, melted
Salt and freshly ground pepper
12 venison loin slices or medallions
    (about 2½ ounces each)
3 tablespoons clarified butter
    (see Note)
2 tablespoons Cointreau or
    Grand Marnier
1 cup pinot noir or other dry, fruity
    red wine
3 paper-thin slices orange, halved
    crosswise
12 dried cranberries

RINSE AN 8 X 12-INCH ROASTING PAN with cold water and shake it dry. Mound the polenta in the pan and, using a rubber spatula repeatedly dipped in very hot water, spread the polenta evenly in the pan until it is just over ¼ inch thick. Cover the pan with a tea towel and allow to rest for 1 hour at room temperature or up to 24 hours in the refrigerator.

WHEN READY TO SERVE, preheat a grill or broiler to high heat.

CUT THE POLENTA into 12 diamond shapes, brush them with the melted butter, and put them under the hot broiler for 4 to 5 minutes on each side, or until golden and crunchy.

SALT AND PEPPER BOTH SIDES of the venison medallions to taste. In a large heavy skillet, heat the clarified butter over medium-high heat and cook the medallions for about 2 to 3 minutes on each side. Be very careful not to overcook; the meat should still have a rosy tinge to it. Remove to a plate in a low oven while you finish the sauce.

IMMEDIATELY TURN UP THE HEAT under the skillet to high and add the Cointreau. Tip the pan to the side so that it catches fire and allow it to flame for 1 minute. Add the remaining 1 cup venison stock and the pinot noir to the pan, putting out the flame, and reduce rapidly until there is only 1 scant cup of slightly syrupy liquid remaining.

PLACE 2 POLENTA DIAMONDS in the center of each of 6 warmed dinner plates and top with a venison medallion. Drizzle the sauce over the top and garnish each plate with half a slice of orange topped with 2 dried cranberries. Serve immediately.

NOTE: To make clarified butter, in a small heavy saucepan melt 8 tablespoons (1 stick) unsalted butter over very low heat. Set the pan aside for 5 minutes. With a spoon, carefully remove and discard the foamy white butterfat from the top, then slowly pour off the clear liquid, leaving the milky residue at the bottom of the pan. (May be refrigerated, covered, for up to 1 month). Makes about 6 tablespoons.

Asides

90   *Sage Polenta Gnocchi*

92   *Fennel-Chèvre Polenta Wedges*

93   *Herbed Polenta Cornsticks*

95   *Lemon and Oregano Polenta Muffins*

96   *Pan-fried Tomatoes with a Cornmeal Crust*

98   *Garlic-Onion Grilled Polenta Squares*

100   *Three-Cheese Soft Polenta*

101   *White Corn and Arugula Timbales*

102   *Röckenwagner's Polenta Fries*

103   *Fennel Seed and Rosemary Breadsticks*

Sage Polenta Gnocchi

This is a substantial but delicious side dish that would go nicely with a simple main course of grilled giant shrimp, cracked crab, or simple Florentine-style steak. Yes, there is butter, cream, and cheese, but you won't eat it every day, right? This recipe is based on a traditional Italian-style gnocchi, generally quite a dense mixture which is cut into shapes and then baked with a sauce. Italian gnocchi are made either with semolina or with potatoes, with many variations in between. SERVES 6

½ cup polenta or coarsely ground
    yellow cornmeal

½ cup coarse semolina

2 cups milk

½ cup water

4 tablespoons (½ stick) unsalted
    butter

1 teaspoon coarse sea salt

¼ teaspoon white pepper

¾ cup freshly grated Parmesan

10 fresh sage leaves, finely chopped,
    or 2 teaspoons dried sage,
    crumbled

¼ cup whipping cream

6 whole sage leaves, for garnish

MIX THE POLENTA and the semolina in a measuring cup. In a medium-size heavy saucepan, combine the milk, water, butter, salt, and pepper and bring the mixture to a boil. Reduce the heat a little and, when the liquid is simmering, pour in the polenta and semolina in a very slow, thin stream, whisking constantly in the same direction until all the grains are incorporated and no lumps remain. Reduce the heat to very low. Switch to a wooden paddle and stir thoroughly every 1 or 2 minutes for 15 to 20 minutes, or until the mixture comes away from the sides of the pan and the grains have just begun to soften. Stir in ½ cup of the Parmesan and the chopped sage.

RINSE AN 8 x 12-INCH ROASTING PAN with water and shake dry. Pour the polenta mixture into the pan and spread into an even layer just under ½ inch thick, smoothing with a spatula repeatedly dipped into very hot water. Cover with a tea towel and allow to rest for at least 1 hour at room temperature and up to 24 hours in the refrigerator.

PREHEAT THE OVEN to 400°F. Lightly oil an oval or rectangular ceramic baking dish, gratin pan, or Pyrex dish.

WITH A 3-INCH ROUND COOKIE CUTTER or glass, cut the polenta into as many circles as possible, then lay them in the baking dish in rows, over-lapping each by about half. Sprinkle the remaining ¼ cup Parmesan over the top and drizzle the cream around the edges and in between the rows.

BAKE FOR 20 TO 25 MINUTES, or until the top is golden brown and the cream is bubbling. Serve from the baking dish set on a heatproof trivet, garnished at the last minute with the whole sage leaves.

Fennel-Chèvre Polenta Wedges

Served after a fifteen-minute rest, these wedges are soft and melting, much like a soufflé.

SERVES 8

Butter, for preparing the pan

2 tablespoons extra virgin olive oil

1 clove garlic, minced

2 medium shallots, finely chopped

1 small bulb fennel, core removed and
  discarded, finely chopped

2 cups milk

3 cups chicken stock, preferably
  homemade (pages 20-21)

1 teaspoon coarse sea salt

1 cup polenta or coarsely ground
  yellow cornmeal

Freshly ground pepper

2 large eggs, separated, at room
  temperature

¼ cup freshly grated Parmesan

¼ cup finely chopped fennel
  greens or dill

2 ounces goat cheese, crumbled

PREHEAT THE OVEN to 425°F. Butter an 8-inch springform pan.

IN A LARGE HEAVY SAUCEPAN, heat the olive oil over medium-low heat. Add the garlic, shallots, and chopped fennel bulb and sauté, stirring occasionally, for 7 to 8 minutes, or until the shallots are translucent. Add the milk, chicken stock, and salt and increase the heat to high. Gradually sprinkle the polenta over in a very slow, thin stream, whisking in the same direction until no lumps remain. Reduce the heat to very low. Switch to a wooden paddle and stir thoroughly every 1 or 2 minutes for 15 to 20 minutes, or until the mixture pulls away from the sides of the pan and the grains of polenta have begun to soften. Remove from the heat. Stir in the pepper, egg yolks, and Parmesan until thoroughly blended.

IN A MIXING BOWL, beat the egg whites to soft peaks. Stir a quarter of the whites thoroughly into the polenta mixture to lighten it, then fold the remaining whites in gently, being sure not to overfold. Spoon one-third of the polenta into the prepared pan in an even layer. Sprinkle half of the chopped fennel greens and half of the goat cheese over the top. Spoon in half of the remaining polenta mixture in an even layer. Sprinkle with the remaining fennel greens and goat cheese and spoon the remaining polenta mixture on top, smoothing with a spatula to make a flat top.

BAKE FOR 25 TO 30 MINUTES, or until the soufflé pulls away from the sides of the pan and the center is firm. Cool on a rack for 15 minutes, run a knife around the edge of the pan to release the soufflé, and remove the sides of the pan. Slice into wedges and serve immediately.

NOTE: To prepare this dish ahead of time, let the soufflé cool completely before removing the pan. When ready to serve, cut into wedges, transfer them to a lightly oiled baking sheet, and reheat in a 425°F oven for 15 to 20 minutes.

Herbed Polenta Cornsticks

If you have cast-iron cornstick pans, these cornsticks make a very festive presentation. I like to wrap them in a calico napkin in a wicker basket and pass them with a little pot of red pepper butter. If you don't have cornstick pans use a muffin pan. The flavor is every bit as good!

MAKES 14 CORNSTICKS

PREHEAT THE OVEN to 425°F. Lightly oil 2 cast-iron cornstick pans. Place the pans in the oven to preheat.

IN A LARGE MIXING BOWL, combine the polenta, flour, baking powder, salt, rosemary, and sugar and stir together with a fork until well mixed. Add the milk, egg, and melted butter and stir together just until mixed. The batter will be a little lumpy and thick. Fold in the chopped basil. Working quickly, pull out the oven shelf and spoon the mixture into the hot pans.

BAKE FOR 15 MINUTES, or until lightly puffed and golden. Remove from the oven and allow to sit for 5 minutes. Serve hot or cool on racks.

Vegetable oil, for preparing pans

1 cup polenta or coarsely ground yellow cornmeal

1 cup all-purpose flour

1 tablespoon baking powder

1 scant teaspoon coarse sea salt

1 teaspoon finely chopped fresh rosemary

2 tablespoons sugar

1 cup milk

1 large egg, lightly beaten

¼ cup unsalted butter, melted

⅓ cup finely chopped fresh basil

Lemon and Oregano
Polenta Muffins

Not your usual muffins by any means, these little gems go perfectly with grilled dishes such as a Greek-style chicken. Add a cucumber and tomato salad and search out a cold bottle of retsina, the pine resin-scented Greek wine. (Sounds strange but tastes like what the Gods would drink, which, come to think of it, it probably was.)

MAKES 12 MUFFINS

PREHEAT THE OVEN to 425°F. Butter a 12-cup standard-size muffin pan thoroughly.

IN A SMALL SKILLET, heat 1 tablespoon of butter over medium heat and sauté the shallot until softened, about 3 to 4 minutes. In a small mixing bowl, sift together the flour, baking powder, baking soda, sugar, and salt. Stir in the polenta with a fork until the dry ingredients are evenly blended. In a large mixing bowl, beat together the eggs, melted butter, sour cream, and milk until well combined. Add the softened shallot, lemon zest, oregano, and the dry ingredients and stir with a fork until just blended. Do not overmix. Divide the batter equally among the muffin cups, filling them all the way up.

BAKE FOR 20 MINUTES, or until puffed and deep golden. Cool on a rack and serve while still slightly warm.

Butter, for preparing the pan

1 tablespoon unsalted butter

1 large shallot, finely chopped

1 cup all-purpose flour

1½ teaspoons baking powder

1 teaspoon baking soda

1 teaspoon sugar

½ teaspoon table salt

¾ cup polenta or coarsely ground yellow cornmeal

2 large eggs, lightly beaten

4 tablespoons (½ stick) unsalted butter, melted and cooled

1 cup sour cream

½ cup milk

1 teaspoon finely chopped lemon zest

2 teaspoons finely chopped fresh oregano or 1 scant teaspoon dried oregano, crumbled

Pan-fried Tomatoes with a Cornmeal Crust

In the American South cornmeal is often used to coat oysters, catfish, and chicken before frying them, but this dish, with its crunchy exterior and red-ripe, smooth tomato inside, becomes very Mediterranean. It would be a waste to use extra virgin olive oil for frying the tomatoes, but regular olive oil will impart more flavor than plain vegetable oil.

SERVES 6

9 large ripe but firm plum tomatoes
  (about 1¾ pounds)
½ cup polenta or coarsely ground
  yellow cornmeal
Salt and freshly ground black pepper
2 tablespoons finely chopped Italian
  parsley
⅓ cup olive oil or vegetable oil

SLICE THE TOMATOES crosswise about ½ inch thick. Discard or eat the very top and bottom slices. Mix the polenta, ½ teaspoon salt, pepper to taste, and parsley in a shallow soup bowl and dredge the tomato slices evenly in the mixture, pressing the coating to make it stick to the cut surfaces of the tomatoes.

IN A LARGE HEAVY NONSTICK SKILLET, heat the oil over medium-high heat until it is very hot but not smoking. Add as many tomato slices as you can without crowding the pan, and sauté for about 3 minutes. Turn the slices to the other side and sauté for another 3 minutes, or until golden. Remove to a paper towel–lined plate, sprinkle with salt, and keep warm in a low oven while you finish frying the other tomatoes. Serve warm.

Garlic-Onion Grilled Polenta Squares

This is the simplest of dishes. It can rest in the pan anywhere from one hour to one day before you cut and grill it, it is redolent of garlic and cheese, and, best of all, it is the perfect partner for my favorite Jody Maroni sausages—Pumante Italian with sun-dried tomatoes, prosciutto, wine, and pine nuts, which you can get by mail order (page 117). I just throw them into a pan with the polenta squares around the sides, and grill it all under the broiler until everything is browned. It's my comfort food. SERVES 6 TO 8

2 tablespoons extra virgin olive oil

2 cloves garlic, finely chopped

½ medium-size red onion, finely chopped

2 cups chicken stock, preferably homemade (pages 20-21)

2 cups water

1 teaspoon coarse sea salt

1 cup polenta or coarsely ground yellow cornmeal

¼ teaspoon freshly ground black pepper

⅓ cup freshly grated Parmesan

2 tablespoons unsalted butter

Olive oil, for brushing

IN A LARGE HEAVY SAUCEPAN, heat the olive oil over low heat. Add the garlic and the red onion and sauté, stirring constantly, for about 3 minutes, or until softened. Do not let the garlic burn. Add the chicken stock, water, and salt and bring to a boil over medium-high heat. Reduce the heat and, when the liquid is simmering, gradually sprinkle the polenta over in a very slow, thin stream, whisking constantly in the same direction until all the grains have been incorporated and no lumps remain. Reduce the heat to very low. Switch to a wooden paddle and stir thoroughly every 1 or 2 minutes for 25 to 30 minutes, or until the mixture pulls away from the sides of the pan and the grains of polenta have softened. Stir in the pepper, Parmesan, and butter. The mixture will be quite thick.

RINSE AN 8 x 12-INCH ROASTING PAN with water and shake dry. Mound the polenta into the pan and, using a rubber spatula repeatedly dipped in very hot water, spread the polenta evenly in the pan until it is just under ½ inch thick. Cover with a tea towel and allow to rest for 1 hour at room temperature or up to 24 hours in the refrigerator.

WHEN READY TO SERVE, preheat a broiler to high heat. Brush the broiler pan with oil.

CUT THE POLENTA into 8 equal squares and brush them with olive oil. Transfer the squares to the broiler pan and grill for about 8 minutes on each side, or until deep golden brown. Serve immediately.

Three-Cheese Soft Polenta

When something is perfect, why change it? My good friend and mentor Evan Kleiman and her partner Vianna LaPlace created this recipe for their wonderful book Cucina Rustica. *Although this is a classic dish, I've never found a better recipe for it. However, I do like to make up the polenta with half stock instead of all water. I feel it adds a more complex flavor without adding any more calories. With a green salad and a bottle of Chianti, this dish makes a perfect dinner for four, or serve it for six alongside grilled lamb loin chops topped with caper butter.* SERVES 4 TO 6

3¼ cups water

3¼ cups chicken stock, preferably
    homemade (pages 20-21)

1 teaspoon coarse sea salt

1½ cups polenta or coarsely ground
    yellow cornmeal

4 tablespoons (½ stick) unsalted
    butter

4 ounces gorgonzola, cut into 1-inch
    chunks

½ pound Italian fontina, cut into
    1-inch chunks

½ cup grated Parmesan

Freshly grated black pepper

Parmesan, for passing (optional)

IN A LARGE HEAVY SAUCEPAN, bring the water and stock to a boil and add the salt. Reduce the heat and, when the liquid is simmering, sprinkle the polenta evenly in a very slow, thin stream, whisking constantly in the same direction until all the grains have been incorporated and no lumps remain. Reduce the heat to very low. Switch to a wooden paddle and stir thoroughly every 1 or 2 minutes for 30 to 40 minutes, or until the mixture pulls away from the sides of the pan and the grains of polenta have softened. Remove from the heat and stir in the butter until it is completely incorporated. Stir in the cheeses. When they have begun to melt, season to taste with black pepper. Serve immediately in individual heated bowls, bringing the Parmesan to pass at the table.

NOTE: Be sure to get Italian fontina cheese for this dish, the kind that is covered with a brown, barklike rind, rather than Swiss fontina, which has a red rind and does not melt as smoothly.

White Corn and Arugula Timbales

The peppery bite of arugula contrasts beautifully with the sweetness of fresh corn.
Have the rest of the dinner prepared by the time the timbales are ready to come out of the oven—they do not wait well.

SERVES 8

PREHEAT THE OVEN to 425°F. Butter eight 5-ounce ceramic or metal ramekins thoroughly and sprinkle them with Parmesan. Set the ramekins in a roasting pan just large enough to hold them all.

IN A MEDIUM SAUCEPAN, bring the milk to a simmer over medium-high heat. Add the corn and simmer for 3 minutes. Strain the milk back into a measuring cup and set the corn aside. Add fresh milk if necessary to make 2 cups.

IN A LARGE HEAVY SAUCEPAN, heat the butter over medium-low heat. Add the garlic and shallots and sauté, stirring occasionally, for 3 to 4 minutes, or until softened. Add the milk, chicken stock, and salt to the saucepan and increase the heat to medium-high. Gradually sprinkle the polenta over in a very slow, thin stream, whisking constantly in the same direction until no lumps remain. Reduce the heat to very low. Switch to a wooden paddle and stir every 1 or 2 minutes for 15 to 20 minutes, or until the mixture pulls away from the sides of the pan and the grains of polenta have begun to soften. Remove from the heat and stir in the pepper, egg yolks, corn, and Parmesan until thoroughly blended.

IN A MIXING BOWL, beat the egg whites to soft peaks. Stir a quarter of the whites thoroughly into the polenta mixture to lighten it, then fold the remaining whites and the chopped arugula in gently, being careful not to overfold. Spoon the polenta into the ramekins, filling them to the top. Pour boiling water into the roasting pan until the water comes halfway up the sides of the ramekins.

BAKE FOR 10 TO 12 MINUTES, or until the centers are firm. Run a small knife around the edges of the ramekins to release the timbales, and turn them out upside down straight onto the dinner plates. Garnish the top of each with a tiny arugula leaf and serve immediately.

Butter and grated Parmesan,
for preparing the ramekins

2 cups milk, or more if necessary

1½ cups white corn kernels
(about 2 ears of corn)

2 tablespoons unsalted butter

1 clove garlic, minced

2 medium shallots, finely chopped

3 cups chicken stock, preferably
homemade (pages 20-21)

1 scant teaspoon coarse sea salt

1 cup polenta or coarsely ground
yellow cornmeal

Freshly ground black pepper

2 large eggs, separated, at room
temperature

⅓ cup freshly grated Parmesan

1½ tablespoons finely chopped
small arugula leaves

8 tiny whole arugula leaves,
for garnish

Röckenwagner's Polenta Fries

Hans Röckenwagner, chef/owner of the restaurant of the same name in Santa Monica, California, was kind enough to contribute this unique recipe for my book. The crunchy golden batons are a revelation. They seem to break some of the most established rules about cooking polenta. For instance, it is only cooked for five minutes, yet is not made with instant polenta. This proves that if you are a classically trained chef, you can do exactly as you please. SERVES 8

2 cups chicken stock, preferably
    homemade (pages 20-21)

2 cups heavy cream

1 teaspoon table salt

½ teaspoon freshly ground
    white pepper

½ tablespoon unsalted butter

½ teaspoon nutmeg

2 cups polenta or coarsely
    ground yellow cornmeal

2 large eggs

1 cup grated Parmesan

Vegetable oil, for deep-frying

LINE AN 8 X 12-INCH ROASTING PAN with parchment paper and set aside.

IN A LARGE HEAVY SAUCEPAN, combine the chicken stock and cream and bring to a boil, watching carefully that the liquid does not boil over. Add the salt, pepper, butter, and nutmeg and reduce the heat. When the liquid is at a simmer, sprinkle in the polenta in a slow, thin stream, whisking constantly in the same direction until all the grains are absorbed and the mixture is smooth. Reduce the heat to low. Switch to a wooden paddle and stir the polenta constantly for 2 to 3 minutes, or until it begins to thicken. Break one of the eggs into the mixture, stirring until it is absorbed. Stir for 1 minute more, then add the remaining egg in the same way. Stir in the Parmesan. The mixture will be very thick and pale yellow. Mound the polenta mixture in the roasting pan using a spatula repeatedly dipped into very hot water and spread the polenta into an even layer just under ½ inch thick. Cover with a tea towel and refrigerate for at least 6 hours or overnight.

WHEN READY TO SERVE, in a large heavy saucepan or deep-fat fryer, heat 4 or 5 inches of oil to 375°F. Cut the polenta into 4 x ¾-inch batons, like cottage fries. Deep-fry the polenta batons for about 4 minutes, or until deep golden brown outside and still pale yellow inside. Transfer to a paper towel–lined plate. You will need to do this in 3 batches, keeping the first batch warm in a low oven while you cook the remaining batches. Make sure to bring the oil back up to 375°F before frying the second and third batches. Serve immediately.

Fennel Seed and Rosemary Breadsticks

When I tested these crunchy breadsticks, with their herb flavor and welcome salty bite, my friend Richard couldn't get over the fact that I'd made them myself. "You really made these?" he repeated several times. Of all the polenta dishes I had tested on him, only these struck a note of incredulity. Maybe it's because a fresh breadstick is usually encountered only in the best Italian restaurants. These come right up to the highest standards. Whether you've worked with yeast before or not, you can reproduce these. You could too, Richard!

MAKES 32 BREADSTICKS

IN A LARGE MEASURING CUP, combine the yeast, sugar, and ½ cup of the water and stir to dissolve. Allow to stand for about 10 minutes, or until the yeast mixture forms a frothy head. (If no head forms, the yeast is bad. Discard the mixture and start again with fresh yeast.) Stir in the remaining ½ cup water and the olive oil.

IN THE BOWL OF A FOOD PROCESSOR fitted with the metal blade, combine the all-purpose flour, whole wheat flour, polenta, rosemary, orange zest, and salt and process in several short bursts to combine. With the motor running, add the yeast mixture through the feed tube in a steady stream, taking about 10 seconds to pour it in. Continue to process for 10 seconds more, by which time the dough should have formed a ball on the stem. If the dough is too wet and forms a ball right away, remove the cover and sprinkle 2 tablespoons of all-purpose flour over the dough. Or if it is too dry and has not formed a ball on the stem within 15 seconds, sprinkle over 1 to 2 tablespoons more water. Process in 5-second bursts 3 more times, then turn the dough out onto a lightly floured board and knead for 1 minute. The dough should be slightly soft but not sticky.

BEGIN STRETCHING, pushing, and pulling the dough with your fingertips and the heel of your hand into an 8 x 12-inch rectangle. This will take a while as the dough will be very tight at first. Be patient: Within about 5 minutes it will soften up and acquiesce. Transfer the dough to a

1 envelope (¼ ounce) active dry yeast

1 teaspoon sugar

1 cup warm water (about 110°F)

¼ cup extra virgin olive oil

2 cups all-purpose flour, or more as needed

½ cup whole wheat flour

½ cup polenta or coarsely ground yellow cornmeal

2 teaspoons finely chopped fresh rosemary

1 teaspoon finely chopped orange zest

1 teaspoon table salt

Olive oil, for rising the dough

1 large egg, beaten

Fennel seeds

Coarse sea salt

Extra virgin olive oil, for serving (optional)

(cont.)

103

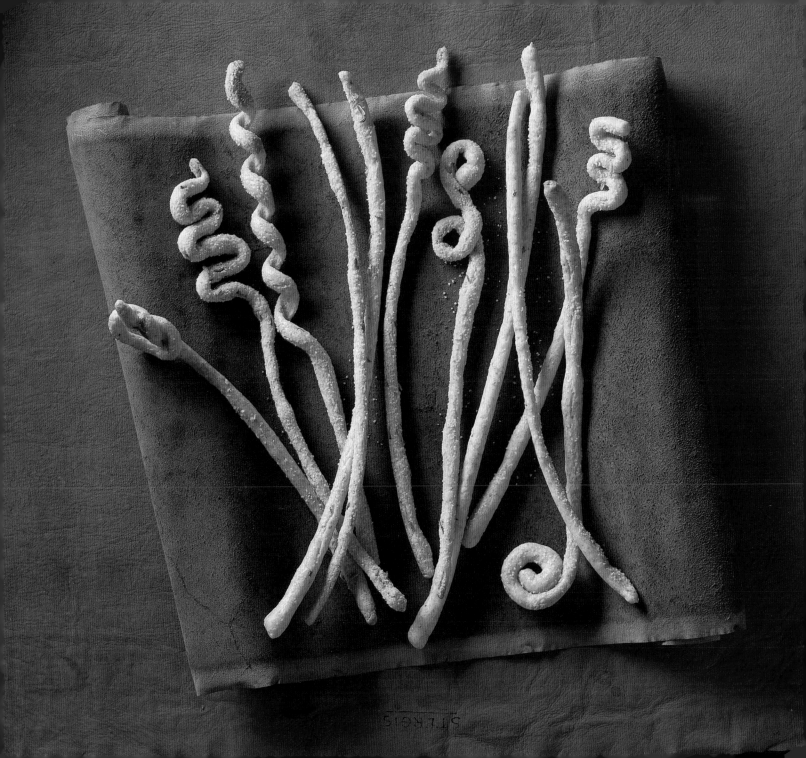

generously oiled baking sheet and brush the top of the dough with more oil. Cover with a tea towel and allow to rise in a warm, draft-free place for about 45 minutes, or until puffy.

PREHEAT THE OVEN to 400°F.

TRANSFER THE DOUGH to an unfloured cutting board and cut it crosswise into 4 equal sections. Cut them crosswise into 8 little strips and roll each one under the palms of your hands into a thin rope about 12 inches long. Transfer to oiled baking sheets. Do this in batches if necessary, keeping the unrolled strips covered with the towel and rolling them out just before baking. Brush with beaten egg and sprinkle with fennel seeds and coarse salt to taste.

BAKE FOR 15 MINUTES, or until slightly golden. Serve warm with a little dish of your best extra virgin olive oil or cool on racks. (The breadsticks will keep in an airtight container for up to 2 weeks. To serve them after they have been stored for a few days, reheat on a dry baking sheet, uncovered, at 350°F for 20 minutes.)

Desserts

107 *Wine-poached Pears on Spicy Polenta Croûtes*

110 *Polenta Pound Cake with Warm Summer Fruits*

113 *Polenta Dolce with Dried Dates and Ricotta*

114 *Cornmeal Tart with Plums and Currants*

Wine-poached Pears
on Spicy Polenta Croûtes

These glistening ruby-red pears are soft and sweet, the polenta croûtes are crunchy and slightly caramelized, and the sauce is rich and unctuous. Best of all, you can make everything ahead of time except for grilling the croûtes. If you are in the mood for a surprise, stuff the bottoms of the pears with cheese.

SERVES 6

TO PREPARE THE PEARS: Cut a slice from the bottom of each pear so that it will stand upright in the poaching pan. Peel the pears from the base toward the stem, leaving the stem intact. In a saucepan just large enough to hold all the pears standing up but no larger, combine the wine with enough water so that the pears will be covered up to the base of the stems. Add the sugar and, over low heat, stir just until the sugar has dissolved. Add the vanilla bean and lemon zest. Place the pears in the wine and bring the liquid to a slow simmer. Simmer, turning occasionally to be sure the pears take on the color of the wine evenly, until they are tender, 15 to 25 minutes, depending on how ripe the pears are. Transfer the poached pears to a plate.

REDUCE THE LIQUID over high heat until it is syrupy. It will thicken further as it cools, so don't reduce it all the way down. Remove the vanilla bean and lemon zest. (Both the pears and the syrup may be refrigerated for up to 24 hours before serving.)

TO MAKE THE POLENTA: In a medium-size heavy saucepan, combine the milk, water, salt, and 1 tablespoon of the sugar and bring the mixture to a boil. Reduce the heat and, when the liquid is simmering, sprinkle in the polenta in a very slow, thin stream, whisking constantly in the same direction until all the grains have been incorporated and no lumps remain. Reduce the heat to very low. Switch to a wooden paddle and stir thoroughly every 1 or 2 minutes for 15 to 20 minutes, or until the mixture

POACHED PEARS
6 firm pears, such as Bosc or
   Conference, just beginning to ripen
1 bottle zinfandel
1 to 2 cups water, as needed
¼ cup sugar, or more, depending on
   the ripeness of the pears
1 vanilla bean
1 long piece of lemon zest

SPICED POLENTA CROÛTES
2 cups milk
1 cup water
½ teaspoon coarse sea salt
2 tablespoons sugar
1 cup polenta or coarsely ground
   yellow cornmeal
2 tablespoons unsalted butter
Generous pinch of ground allspice
Generous pinch of ground cloves
Generous pinch of ground ginger

(cont.)

comes away from the sides of the pan and the grains of polenta have begun to soften. Stir in the butter, allspice, cloves, and ginger and remove from the heat. The mixture will be so thick that the paddle will stand upright for 2 or 3 seconds.

RINSE AN 8 x 4½-INCH LOAF PAN with cold water and shake dry. Mound the polenta into the pan, smoothing the top with a spatula repeatedly dipped into very hot water. Cover with a tea towel and allow to rest for at least 2 hours at room temperature or up to 24 hours in the refrigerator.

RUN A KNIFE around the edge of the loaf pan to loosen the polenta and invert it on a cutting board. Cut the polenta into twelve ¾-inch slices and let them dry on a rack for 1 hour.

WHEN READY TO SERVE, preheat the broiler to high heat.

GRILL THE SLICES for 7 minutes on 1 side, or until they have just started to turn golden. Turn to the other side and sprinkle each one evenly with ¼ teaspoon of the remaining sugar. Grill for 6 minutes more, until the sugar is bubbling and caramelized, watching carefully to be sure that the sugar does not burn. Transfer 2 croûtes, browned side up, to each of 6 warmed dessert plates and place a poached pear in between the croûtes. Drizzle about 1 tablespoon of the syrup over the stem of each pear and serve immediately.

VARIATION: Mix 3 tablespoons each gorgonzola and heavy cream. Cradle a poached pear in 1 hand and carefully scoop out the core with a melon baller. Fill the cavity with the cheese, smooth off the bottom, and place standing up on the plate so that the filling is completely unsuspected.

Polenta Pound Cake with Warm Summer Fruits

This golden cake is dense and slightly crunchy, not a lighter-than-air pound cake, though it certainly looks like one. Topped with a warm fruit ragout and a dollop of cool sweetened mascarpone, it makes a wonderfully sunny dessert.

SERVES 6 TO 8

POLENTA POUND CAKE

½ pound (2 sticks) unsalted butter, at room temperature

¾ cup superfine sugar

¼ teaspoon table salt

1 teaspoon vanilla extract

3 large eggs, at room temperature

3 large egg yolks, at room temperature

1½ cups all-purpose flour

½ cup medium-grind yellow cornmeal

1 teaspoon baking powder

WARM FRUIT RAGOUT

2 tablespoons crème de cassis

2 tablespoons apple juice

1 tablespoon superfine sugar

2 ripe plums, stoned and cut into ⅛-inch slices

2 ripe nectarines, stoned and cut into ⅛-inch slices

2 cups blackberries

⅓ cup mascarpone mixed with 1 teaspoon superfine sugar, for garnish (see Note)

PREHEAT THE OVEN to 350°F. Butter a 9 x 5-inch loaf pan and dredge it with polenta, shaking out the excess.

TO MAKE THE CAKE: In a stand mixer or with a strong hand mixer, cream the butter, sugar, and salt together until light and fluffy. Add the vanilla. Add the eggs and egg yolks, one at a time, completely incorporating each one before adding the next. Sift in the flour, polenta, and baking powder and mix well. Pour the batter into the pan.

BAKE FOR 50 TO 55 MINUTES, or until the top springs back and a skewer inserted in the center comes out clean. Run a knife around the pan to release the cake and invert it onto a rack. Allow to cool completely.

TO PREPARE THE FRUIT: In a medium saucepan, combine the crème de cassis with the apple juice and sugar. Stir over low heat until the sugar has dissolved. Increase the heat and bring the mixture to a boil. Add the plums, nectarines, and blackberries and reduce the heat to a simmer. Cover and simmer for 8 to 10 minutes, or until the fruits are tender. Remove the lid and simmer for 6 to 7 minutes more, stirring occasionally, until the syrup has reduced to coating consistency and the softened fruits are glazed with it.

CUT THE CAKE into 1-inch slices, place on individual dessert plates, and spoon some of the warm fruit and syrup over each. Top with a dollop of sweetened mascarpone and serve.

NOTE: Sweetened crème fraîche or whipped cream may be substituted for the mascarpone.

Polenta Dolce
with Dried Dates and Ricotta

This is a rich, warm, comforting dessert, reminiscent of pudding but without the eggs. It is not too sweet and makes a fine light finish for a slightly heavy meal.
SERVES 6

IN A LARGE HEAVY SAUCEPAN, bring the milk, water, salt, and sugar to a boil over medium-high heat, watching carefully that the milk doesn't boil over. Reduce the heat so that the liquid is barely simmering and drizzle the polenta over in a slow, thin stream, whisking constantly in the same direction until all the grains have been absorbed and the mixture is lumpfree. Reduce the heat to very low. Switch to a wooden paddle and stir thoroughly every 1 or 2 minutes for 25 to 30 minutes, or until the polenta pulls away from the sides of the pan and the grains have softened. Stir in the butter and Grand Marnier. It should be a fairly loose mixture.

IMMEDIATELY MOUND THE SOFT POLENTA into heated dessert bowls and make an impression in the middle with the back of the paddle. Place a dollop of the sweetened ricotta in the center of each hollow, scatter with chopped dates, and sprinkle with allspice.

VARIATION: Substitute mixed berries for the dates and replace the allspice with vanilla sugar.

3 cups milk

1 cup water

½ teaspoon coarse sea salt

3 tablespoons sugar

1 cup polenta or coarsely ground yellow cornmeal

2 tablespoons unsalted butter

1 tablespoon Grand Marnier or Cointreau

½ cup ricotta cheese, whisked together with 1 tablespoon sugar

¾ cup seeded and coarsely chopped dates

Pinch of ground allspice

Cornmeal Tart with Plums and Currants

This is definitely a summer tart, and I like to eat it with a full-cream lemon ice cream—if you can find one amidst all the low-fat products that most markets seem to carry these days! SERVES 6 TO 8

CORNMEAL CRUST

2 cups all-purpose flour

½ cup medium-grind yellow cornmeal

⅓ cup sugar

1 teaspoon baking powder

½ teaspoon table salt

12 tablespoons (1½ sticks) cold
   unsalted butter, cubed

1 large egg

1 large egg yolk

¼ teaspoon ground cinnamon

1 tablespoon dry white wine, if
   needed

PLUM AND CURRANT FILLING

12 ripe black plums, stoned and cut
   into eighths

¼ teaspoon ground cinnamon

⅔ cup sugar, or more if the plums are
   not quite ripe

1½ tablespoons Cognac or Armagnac

⅔ cup dried currants

1 pint lemon ice cream, for serving
   (optional)

TO MAKE THE CRUST: In a food processor, combine the flour, polenta, sugar, baking powder, and salt and process just to mix. Add the butter and process in short bursts, scraping down the sides of the bowl as necessary, until the mixture resembles coarse bread crumbs. Add the whole egg, egg yolk, and cinnamon and process again in short bursts, scraping down the sides, until the dough just comes together, but is still a bit crumbly. Add a little of the wine only if the dough seems very dry. Do not overprocess or the crust will be tough. Turn the dough out onto a lightly floured surface, work it together into a ball, press it down into a disk, and wrap with plastic. Refrigerate for at least 1 hour or overnight.

TO MAKE THE FILLING: In a medium saucepan combine the plums, cinnamon, sugar, Cognac, and currants. Stir together over low heat until the sugar has dissolved, then cover and simmer for about 15 minutes, or until the plums are very soft. Set aside to cool, uncovered.

PREHEAT THE OVEN to 350°F. Line a 12-inch tart pan with high sides and a removable bottom with parchment paper.

ON A LIGHTLY FLOURED SURFACE, roll out the pastry to a 14-inch round, letting it rest for 5 minutes if it is difficult to roll when it first comes out of the refrigerator. Line the tart pan with the dough, pressing it into the corners and up the sides and patching it if necessary. Set the pan on a baking sheet and spoon the filling into the tart shell.

BAKE FOR ABOUT 45 MINUTES, or until the filling is bubbly and the crust is golden. Cool on a rack for 15 minutes. Remove the sides of the pan. Serve either slightly warm or at room temperature, with a scoop of lemon ice cream, if desired.

Bibliography

Ash, John and Sid Goldstein. *American Game Cooking*. Reading, MA: Aris Books, 1991.

Bailey, Lee. *California Wine Country Cooking*. New York: Clarkson Potter, 1991.

Beard, James. *The New James Beard*. New York: Alfred A. Knopf, 1981.

Bugialli, Giuliano. *Foods of Tuscany*. New York: Stewart, Tabori & Chang, 1984.

———. *The Fine Art of Italian Cooking*. New York: Random House, 1986.

Child, Julia. *The Way to Cook*. New York: Alfred A. Knopf, 1993.

David, Elizabeth. *Italian Food*. Middlesex: Penguin Books, 1954.

Dodi, Andrea and Hedy Giusti-Lanham. *The Best of Northern Italian Cooking*. New York: Barron's, 1978.

Ellmer, Bruno. *Classical and Contemporary Italian Cooking for Professionals*. New York: Van Nostrand Reinhold, 1990.

Field, Carol. *Celebrating Italy*. New York: William Morrow & Co., 1990.

Field, Michael and Frances. *Foods of the World: A Quintet of Cuisines*. New York: Time-Life Books, 1970.

Gilbertie, Sal. *Kitchen Herbs*. New York: Bantam Books, 1988.

The Good Cook: Game (European English Edition). Amsterdam: Time-Life Books, 1980.

The Good Cook: Grains, Pasta & Pulses (European English Edition). Amsterdam: Time-Life Books, 1980.

The Good Cook: Lamb (European English Edition). Amsterdam: Time-Life Books, 1980.

Hazan, Marcella. *Marcella's Italian Kitchen*. New York: Alfred A. Knopf, 1986.

———. *The Classic Italian Cookbook*. New York: Alfred A. Knopf, 1979.

Kasper, Lynne Rossetto. *The Splendid Table*. New York: William Morrow & Co., 1992.

Kleiman, Evan and Vianna LaPlace. *Cucina Rustica*. New York: William Morrow & Co., 1990.

London, Sheryl and Mel. *The Versatile Grain and the Elegant Bean*. New York: Simon & Schuster, 1992.

McGee, Harold. *On Food and Cooking*. New York: Charles Scribner's Sons, 1984.

Papashvily, Helen and George. *Foods of the World: Russian Cooking*. New York: Time-Life Books, 1969.

Root, Waverley. *The Food of Italy*. New York: Atheneum, 1971.

Scicolone, Michele. *La Dolce Vita*. New York: William Morrow & Co., 1993.

Taylor, John Martin. *Hoppin' John's Low Country Cooking*. New York: Bantam Books, 1992.

van der Post, Laurens. *Foods of the World: African Cooking*. New York: Time-Life Books, 1970.

Walter, Eugene. *Foods of the World: American Cooking: Southern Style*. New York: Time-Life Books, 1971.

Wheaton, Barbara Ketcham. *Savouring the Past*. London: Chatto & Windus, 1983.

Wolfe, Linda. *Foods of the World: The Cooking of the Caribbean Islands*. New York: Time-Life Books, 1970.

Mail-Order Sources

Balducci's
424 Avenue of the Americas
New York, NY 10011
(800) 225-3822
Baretta Polenta

Dean & Deluca Importers, Inc.
560 Broadway
New York, NY 10012
(800) 221-7714
Come una Volta polenta, Polenta Tarragona (polenta nera), Polenta Integra (coarse cornmeal with the germ)

Jody Maroni's Sausage Kingdom
2011 Ocean Front Walk
Venice, CA 90291
(800) HAUT-DOG
Chicken and duck sausage with basil, sun-dried tomatoes and Parmesan; Pumante Italian sausage with sun-dried tomatoes, prosciutto, wine, and pine nuts; plus 22 more wildly flavored reduced-fat sausages

Sur La Table
84 Pine Street
Pike Place Farmers Market
Seattle, WA 98101
(800) 243-0852
Copper polenta pot

Zingerman's
422 Detroit Street
Ann Arbor, MI 48106-1868
(313) 769-1625
Fax: (313) 769-1235
Molino e Frantoio polenta, sun-dried tomatoes, dried mushrooms, French sea salt, olive oils and olives, breads, cheeses, etc.

Index

Apple and Dried Cherry Fritters, 28
Apple Compote, 32
Artichoke and Lamb Stew with Oregano Polenta
    Dumplings, 69–70
Arugula and White Corn Timbales, 101

Baby Greens with Blood Oranges and
    Sage-Prosciutto Polenta Croutons, 44, 46
Bacon
    Skewered Chicken Livers, Bacon, and Mush-
        rooms over Polenta Squares, 77–78
    Skillet Cornbread with Corn, Bacon, and
        Jack Cheese, 27
Baked Polenta with Eggplant, Sun-dried Tomatoes
    and Basil Sauce, 41, 43
Bananas and Clover Honey, Polentina with, 29
Beef Short Ribs, Braised, over Soft Polenta with
    Thyme, 71–72
Blueberries and Crème Fraîche, Pancakes with, 31
Braised Beef Short Ribs over Soft Polenta with
    Thyme, 71–72
Breadsticks, Fennel Seed and Rosemary, 103, 105
Bricked Game Hens with Savoy Cabbage on
    Polenta Croûtes, 74–76
Butter, clarified, 88

Cabbage
    Bricked Game Hens with Savoy Cabbage on
        Polenta Croûtes, 74–76
    Cabbage-wrapped Torta with Leeks and
        Pancetta, 58–59
Cheese
    Cabbage-wrapped Torta with Leeks and
        Pancetta, 58–59
    Deep-fried Polenta Sandwiches with
        Spinach and Gorgonzola, 52–53
    Fennel-Chèvre Polenta Wedges, 92
    Gorgonzola Puffs, 60
    Grilled Polenta Crostini with Smoked Trout
        and Mascarpone, 48, 50
    Polenta Dolce with Dried Dates and
        Riccota, 113

Polenta Lasagne with Spinach, Zucchini,
    Herbs, and Fontina, 79, 81
Polenta with Shiitake Mushrooms,
    Mascarpone, and Salmon Roe, 54
Rosemary-Olive Pizzettas with Prosciutto,
    37–38
Skillet Cornbread with Corn, Bacon, and
    Jack Cheese, 27
Three-Cheese Soft Polenta, 100
Cherries
    Apple and Dried Cherry Fritters, 28
Chicken
    Chicken Pot Pie with Cornmeal Crust,
        85–86
    Chicken Stock, 20
    Quick Chicken Stock, 21
    Skewered Chicken Livers, Bacon, and Mush-
        rooms over Polenta Squares, 77–78
Cinnamon Popovers, 32
Corn
    Skillet Cornbread with Corn, Bacon, and
        Jack Cheese, 27
    White Corn and Arugula Timbales, 101
Cornmeal Crust, 85
Cornmeal Tart with Plums and Currants, 114
Cornsticks, Herbed Polenta, 93
Crabmeat Polenta with Lemon and Chive Sauce,
    40
Cranberry-Orange Polenta Diamonds, Venison
    Medallions on, 87
Crostini, Grilled Polenta, with Smoked Trout and
    Mascarpone, 48, 50
Croutons
    Polenta Croutons, 55
    Sage-Prosciutto Polenta Croutons, 44
Currants, Cornmeal Tart with Plums and, 114

Dates, Polenta Dolce with Riccota and, 113
Deep-fried Polenta Sandwiches with Spinach and
    Gorgonzola, 52–53
Desserts
    Cornmeal Tart with Plums and Currants, 114
    Polenta Dolce with Dried Dates and
        Riccota, 113
    Polenta Pound Cake with Warm Summer
        Fruits, 110

Wine-poached Pears on Spicy Polenta
    Croûtes, 107, 109
Duck Breasts with Port Sauce and Wild
    Mushroom Polenta, 63–64
Dumplings, Oregano Polenta, 70

Eggplant, Sun-dried Tomatoes and Basil Sauce,
    Baked Polenta with, 41, 43
Eggs, Poached, Polenta with Smoked Salmon,
    Chives, and, 23
Equipment, 15–16

Fennel-Chèvre Polenta Wedges, 92
Fennel Seed and Rosemary Breadsticks, 103, 105
Fish. See Salmon; Trout
Fried Polenta Squares with Golden Raisins and
    Maple Syrup, 24
Fritters, Apple and Dried Cherry, 28
Fruit. See also individual fruits
    Cornmeal Tart with Plums and Currants, 114
    Polenta Pound Cake with Warm Summer
        Fruits, 110

Game Hens, Bricked, with Savoy Cabbage on
    Polenta Croûtes, 74–76
Garlic-Onion Grilled Polenta Squares, 98
Gnocchi, Sage Polenta, 90
Gorgonzola Puffs, 60
Greens
    Baby Greens with Blood Oranges and Sage-
        Prosciutto Polenta Croutons, 44, 46
    Lentils and Greens in Broth with Polenta
        Croutons, 55–56
Grilled Polenta Crostini with Smoked Trout and
    Mascarpone, 48, 50
Grits, 14

Herbed Polenta Cornsticks, 93

Kumquat Compote, Prune-, 34

Lamb and Artichoke Stew with Oregano Polenta
    Dumplings, 69–70
Lasagne, Polenta, with Spinach, Zucchini, Herbs,
    and Fontina, 79, 81
Leeks and Pancetta, Cabbage-wrapped Torta with,
    58–59

Lemon and Chive Sauce, 40
Lemon and Oregano Polenta Muffins, 95
Lentils and Greens in Broth with Polenta
Croutons, 55–56

Muffins, Lemon and Oregano Polenta, 95
Mushrooms
Duck Breasts with Port Sauce and Wild
Mushroom Polenta, 63–64
Polenta with Shiitake Mushrooms,
Mascarpone, and Salmon Roe, 54
Skewered Chicken Livers, Bacon, and Mush-
rooms over Polenta Squares, 77–78
Soft Polenta with Braised Italian Sausage,
Oven-roasted Tomatoes, and Swiss Chard,
66, 68
Wild Mushroom Ragout, 51

Oranges
Baby Greens with Blood Oranges and Sage-
Prosciutto Polenta Croutons, 44, 46
Venison Medallions on Cranberry-Orange
Polenta Diamonds, 87
Oregano Polenta Dumplings, 70

Pan-fried Tomatoes with a Cornmeal Crust, 96
Pan-fried Trout with Crunchy Polenta Crust, 82
Pancakes with Blueberries and Crème Fraîche, 31
Pancetta, Cabbage-wrapped Torta with Leeks and,
58–59
Pears, Wine-poached, on Spicy Polenta Croûtes,
107, 109
Pizzettas, Rosemary-Olive, with Prosciutto, 37–38
Plums and Currants, Cornmeal Tart with, 114
Polenta
cooking time, 12–13
cornmeal vs., 12
double boiler, 18
holding soft, 18
instant, 13
microwave, 18
nutrition of, 14
problems, 19
stirring, 12–13, 17
technique, 16–18
varieties of, 13–14

Polenta Croutons, 55
Polenta Dolce with Dried Dates and Riccota, 113
Polenta Lasagne with Spinach, Zucchini, Herbs,
and Fontina, 79, 81
Polenta Pound Cake with Warm Summer Fruits,
110
Polenta with Poached Eggs, Smoked Salmon, and
Chives, 23
Polenta with Shiitake Mushrooms, Mascarpone,
and Salmon Roe, 54
Polentina with Bananas and Clover Honey, 29
Popovers, Cinnamon, 32
Pound Cake, Polenta, with Warm Summer Fruits,
110
Prosciutto
Rosemary-Olive Pizzettas with Prosciutto,
37–38
Sage-Prosciutto Polenta Croutons, 44
Prune-Kumquat Compote, 34

Quick Chicken Stock, 21

Röckenwagner's Polenta Fries, 102
Rosemary-Olive Pizzettas with Prosciutto, 37–38

Sage Polenta Gnocchi, 90
Sage-Prosciutto Polenta Croutons, 44
Salmon
Polenta with Poached Eggs, Smoked Salmon,
and Chives, 23
Polenta with Shiitake Mushrooms,
Mascarpone, and Salmon Roe, 54
Sandwiches, Deep-fried Polenta, with Spinach
and Gorgonzola, 52–53
Sausage
Soft Polenta with Braised Italian Sausage,
Oven-roasted Tomatoes, and Swiss Chard,
66, 68
Sautéed Polenta Rounds, 34–35
Skewered Chicken Livers, Bacon, and Mushrooms
over Polenta Squares, 77–78
Skillet Cornbread with Corn, Bacon, and Jack
Cheese, 27
Soft Polenta with Braised Italian Sausage, Oven-
roasted Tomatoes, and Swiss Chard, 66, 68
Soft Polenta with White Truffles and Crème
Fraîche, 47

Spinach
Deep-fried Polenta Sandwiches with Spinach
and Gorgonzola, 52–53
Polenta Lasagne with Spinach, Zucchini,
Herbs, and Fontina, 79, 81
Stock
Chicken Stock, 20
Quick Chicken Stock, 21
Venison Stock, 87
Swiss Chard, Soft Polenta with Braised Italian
Sausage, Oven-roasted Tomatoes, and, 66, 68

Three-Cheese Soft Polenta, 100
Tomato Sauce, 53
Tomatoes
Baked Polenta with Eggplant, Sun-dried
Tomatoes and Basil Sauce, 41, 43
Oven-roasted Tomatoes, 66
Pan-fried Tomatoes with a Cornmeal Crust, 96
Trout
Grilled Polenta Crostini with Smoked Trout
and Mascarpone, 48, 50
Pan-fried Trout with Crunchy Polenta Crust,
82
Truffles, White, Soft Polenta with Crème Fraîche
and, 47

Venison Medallions on Cranberry-Orange Polenta
Diamonds, 87

White Corn and Arugula Timbales, 101
Wild Mushroom Ragout, 51
Wine-poached Pears on Spicy Polenta Croûtes,
107, 109

Zucchini, Polenta Lasagne with Spinach, Herbs,
Fontina, and, 79, 81

Table of Equivalents

The exact equivalents in the following tables have been rounded for convenience.

Fahrenheit	Celsius	Gas
250	120	½
275	140	1
300	150	2
325	160	3
350	180	4
375	190	5
400	200	6
425	220	7
450	230	8
475	240	9
500	260	10

US/UK

oz=ounce
lb=pound
in=inch
ft=foot
tbl=tablespoon
fl oz=fluid ounce
qt=quart

Metric

g=gram
kg=kilogram
mm=millimeter
cm=centimeter
ml=milliliter
l=liter

LIQUIDS

US	Metric	UK
2 tbl	30 ml	1 fl oz
¼ cup	60 ml	2 fl oz
⅓ cup	80 ml	3 fl oz
½ cup	125 ml	4 fl oz
⅔ cup	160 ml	5 fl oz
¾ cup	180 ml	6 fl oz
1 cup	250 ml	8 fl oz
1½ cups	375 ml	12 fl oz
2 cups	500 ml	16 fl oz
4 cups/1 qt	1 l	32 fl oz

WEIGHTS

US/UK	Metric
1 oz	30 g
2 oz	60 g
3 oz	90 g
4 oz (¼ lb)	125 g
5 oz (⅓ lb)	155 g
6 oz	185 g
7 oz	220 g
8 oz (½ lb)	250 g
10 oz	315 g
12 oz (¾ lb)	375 g
14 oz	440 g
16 oz (1 lb)	500 g
1½ lb	750 g
2 lb	1 kg
3 lb	1.5 kg